SCHUBERT LIVES

HOW SCHUBERT'S GREATEST WORKS WERE
SAVED FROM OBLIVION

JOHN UFF

Copyright © 2024 by John Uff

All rights reserved.

No part of this book may be reproduced in any form or by any electronic or mechanical means, including information storage and retrieval systems, without written permission from the author, except for the use of brief quotations in a book review.

CONTENTS

List of Illustrations	v
Foreword	vii
Introduction	ix
PART I LIFE AND DEATH	1
1. Then And Now	3
2. A Short Life	12
3. The Aftermath	30
4. Ferdinand Schubert	37
PART II REAWAKENING	55
5. Three Composers	57
6. The Viennese Schubertians	68
7. Into the 1850s	75
8. The 1860s: A Biography and a Symphony	82
9. And Did Those Feet …	91
PART III REVELATION	103
10. The 1870s and Beyond	105
11. Collecting the works	114
12. The Centenary – A Chance To Reflect	121
13. The twentieth century and today	130
PART IV THE WORKS	147
14. The Piano Works	149
15. The Lieder	160
16. The masses and the operas	176
17. The symphonies	189
PART V EPILOGUE	203
18. Schubert and other composers	205
19. Notable Schubertians	215
20. Has the real Schubert yet emerged?	228
21. Conclusion	243
Bibliography	250
Index	252
About the Author	257

LIST OF ILLUSTRATIONS

1. Schubert's first grave at Währing Cemetery, photograph (2004) p5

2. Lichtenthal Parish Church, postcard from the Morris Collection (c. 1800) p13

3. Franz von Schober, drawing by Leopold Kupelwieser (1821) p16

4. Johann Michael Vogl, lithograph by Josef Kriehuber (1830) p18

5. A portrait by Leopold Kupelwieser, dated by Schubert himself (1821) p21

6. Josef von Spaun, oil painting by Leopold Kupelwieser (1835) p32

7. Ferdinand Schubert in later life, lithograph by Josef Kriehuber (1850) p38

8. A bust of Felix Mendelssohn, the first conductor to perform the *Great* C Major Symphony, author photograph (2024) p64

9. The English translation of von Hellborn's biography, published in two volumes in 1869 p86

10. Sir Augustus Manns, postcard photograph, London, (c. 1900) p92

11. Sir Charles Hallé, photograph by Barraud, Liverpool (c. 1890) p93

12. Sir George Grove p94

13. The Schubert Denkmal, photograph (2019) p105

14. Schubert at the Piano, photograph of the 1899 painting by Gustav Klimt p106

15. Schubert's new grave in the Zentralfriedhof, author photograph (2017) p111

16. Commemorative card for 1928, postcard from the Morris Collection p122

17. A popular depiction of Schubert, postcard from the Morris Collection (c. 1895) p126

LIST OF ILLUSTRATIONS

18. Schubert himself in procession in Vienna in around 1928, postcard from the Morris Collection p130

19. A male-voice part song performed in front of Schubert's final resting place at the Zentralfriedhof, postcard from the Morris Collection (c. 1928) p163

20. The final bars of Der Wegweiser in Schubert's manuscript with the words 'Eine Strasse muss ich gehen die noch keine ging zurück' p170

21. Schubert appearing in Lilac Time, postcard from the Morris Collection (c. 1925) p186

22. The opening of the development section in the finale of the *Great* C Major symphony where a pair of clarinets in E flat give out the theme from Beethoven's Choral Symphony p206

23. Maurice J. E. Brown, family photograph p217

24. John Reed, family photograph p219

25. Professor Brian Newbould, personal photograph p220

Grateful acknowledgement is due for the use of illustrations from the following sources: the Morris Collection (2, 16, 17, 18, 19, 21); National Library of France (5); the family of Maurice J. E. Brown (23); the family of John Reed (24); Professor Brian Newbould (25); author's collection (8, 9, 15); Herbert Josl, an unchanged photograph used under the Creative Commons license, https://commons.wikimedia.org/wiki/File:Währinger_Ortsfriedhof_original_Schubert-Grabstein.jpg (1); Benoît Prieur, an unchanged photograph used under the Creative Commons license, https://commons.wikimedia.org/wiki/File:Monument_%C3%A0_Schubert,_Stadtpark_(Vienne)_ao%C3%BBt_2019_(2).jpg (13); the following images are in the public domain (3, 4, 6, 7, 10, 11, 12, 14).

Every effort has been made to ensure we have not included any copyright material or, where appropriate, have obtained the necessary permissions. If we have made a mistake please contact us and we will remove any infringing images.

FOREWORD

I have had Schubert's music fixed in my head for a very long time – in fact since being a boy treble at school and first encountering, at that time quite unaware who he was or had been, his setting of Psalm 23. Something lodged itself in my mind and has never left. Similarly with other pieces encountered over the years until the realisation that this was the man whose music filled recital rooms, who had died before reaching the age of 32. Yet all the books on the composer and his music seemed to stop in 1828 or perhaps 1865 with the emergence of the *Unfinished* Symphony. How we got from there to an overflowing Wigmore Hall remained a mystery which this book aims to explore.

In the course of the journey from Psalm 23 to the whole vast gamut of Schubert's astonishing output of compositions, I have encountered many like-minded enthusiasts, musicians both amateur and professional, who have been happy to converse and offer ideas which have guided the composition of this book. Many of these have been members of the Schubert Institute (UK) from which body I should mention particularly the generous support of Prof Brian Newbould, Richard Morris, Paul Reed, 'Thea Morris, Lisa Moore and members of the family of the late Maurice Brown and the late John Reed who provided their photographs for this volume. I was not privileged to meet either Maurice or John but, as devoted amateurs, they epitomise the great contribution which English Schubertians have made to the advancement of knowledge and appreciation of this endlessly fascinating composer. They justify the seemingly bold assumption that a book about an Austrian composer of two centuries ago can be written by an amateur English enthusiast.

I must also acknowledge the unfailing support and encouragement of my daughter Leonora Meriel who has given generously of her time and expertise in bringing this work to completion and in surmounting the many hurdles that lie between the thought of writing a book and its appearance in smart covers. The experience of writing books on law did little to prepare me for the outside world of general publishing. I must also acknowledge the special generosity of Richard Morris in not only reading and commenting on the manuscript in draft, but in making his huge collection of Schubert-themed postcards available for use in this book, many of which are unique and not available through any other source. I am also greatly indebted to Brian Newbould whose generous advice included answering the question whether anyone else had written on the subject of what happened to the manuscripts after Schubert's untimely death. The search for records of early performances of the music was most obligingly answered by the Wigmore Hall librarian Emily Woolf. But last and foremost, I must thank Richard Stokes for his searching criticism of the manuscript and for many corrections and improvements. Richard and I were first acquainted through Westminster School where he taught my sons and introduced them to Schubert. It was therefore a great pleasure and opportunity to find his career expanding to become Professor of Lieder at the Royal Academy of Music. I can only say that the book would undoubtedly have been improved had I followed all his advice.

Gray's Inn
February 2025

INTRODUCTION

Franz Schubert was unique as a composer in so many ways. He died before his 32nd birthday, compared to Mozart at 36, Beethoven at 57 and Haydn at 77. Yet he was the most prolific of all the well-known composers, writing a vast treasury of music which, after his early death, took a further 60 years to unearth and catalogue. He had not adopted the practice of other composers of keeping a formal record of the works composed, and often left his manuscripts – of which there might be no other copy – with friends, some of whom proved to be unreliable. While he was an accomplished performer, especially on the piano, he was no virtuoso and was often content to leave it to others to perform his works.

He was also hopeless as a businessman and lived in relative poverty while others, especially publishers, made increasing profits from his works. In contrast to other composers of the early nineteenth century such as Beethoven, Liszt and Mendelssohn who each cultivated the celebrity style, Schubert lived out his days in obscurity. He adopted and perhaps even invented the Bohemian life, preferring the company of poets and artists. His songs with piano gained a dedicated following among a small circle of enthusiasts in Austria, and this included a few prominent individuals and even minor aristocracy. But he never, as Haydn did for many years, held any official post, nor, as Beethoven did, acquired a patron who was in a position to promote his interests. He died in the simple obscurity in which he had lived.

Schubert's music gives pleasure and satisfaction to so many through its particular qualities, which make it instantly identifiable. Many authors and commentators have attempted to describe and define those qualities in terms of harmony and melody. There is very little material in this volume that seeks to add to those attempts, and none which claims to be definitive. In the end one must conclude that there is an intangible element in the music itself (of course) which defies further analysis.

This book describes the slow discovery of the musical gems that Schubert left at his death and which took so long to unearth. That process was, naturally, driven by the extraordinary originality of the works, but it was only in the second half of the nineteenth century, over 20 years after his death, that researchers began to discover who Schubert was, as well as collect together his works. Those tasks occupied the rest of the nineteenth century, and serious Schubert scholarship only properly commenced in the twentieth century.

Schubert studies have now taken root in academic institutions throughout Europe and the United States and particularly in Britain. Here, following the early pioneering work of Sir George Grove and others, a number of Schubert authorities have been able to publish important studies on Schubert's life and music, as well as continuing the process of cataloguing the works. The twentieth and twenty-first centuries have also seen the most profound changes in the dissemination of music from the gramophone to radio and then successive electronic inventions, which have now made great music accessible at the touch of a screen. So Schubert's music is now universally available; many works are now being offered in a host of different performances and include completions of the works which the composer himself left uncomplete.

This profusion of availability has not had the effect some feared, which was the death of live performances. In fact quite the reverse has happened. Concert halls remain in robust business and great music in all its forms commands growing audiences, whose ready access to music has resulted in an increased demand for their music of choice. This has resulted in more artists specialising in great music, including the *lieder* and chamber works of Schubert, in response to the demand of audiences. This is the story of how that demand has developed and grown over the past two centuries.

PART I LIFE AND DEATH

CHAPTER 1
THEN AND NOW

A DEATH

At 3 o'clock on Wednesday the 19 November 1828, on a wintry afternoon, in the second-floor apartment of his elder brother Ferdinand in the south-western suburbs of Vienna, Franz Peter Schubert died, still two months short of his 32nd birthday. The immediate cause of death was certified as nervous fever (*Nervenfieber*) and a contributor was likely to have been a form of typhus, which had given rise to hallucinations and violent delirium in the previous few days. The details of his last illness and death were quickly obscured by conflicting accounts supplied by Ferdinand, for there was an undoubted underlying cause of the death. In about 1822 Franz contracted syphilis, for which he had received treatment on several occasions, including spells in hospital. Syphilis was then incurable and the symptoms were treated with mercury which, being a poison, gave rise to its own problems. By 1828 the disease was in its tertiary stage and may have contributed to the disturbed behaviour; and Franz would also have been suffering from mercury poisoning. The Schubert family had, irrespective of Franz's local celebrity as a composer, been growing in respectability in Vienna, so it was understandable that there should be no report of the true illness.

In many ways it was a good death, given that this was a life cut short by syphilis. In the following decades of the nineteenth century the inheritors of Schubert's genius for *lieder* composition, Robert Schumann and Hugo Wolf, each died from the same underlying cause in pathetic and demeaning circumstances, their reputations temporarily sullied by the manner of their demise. Not so with Franz Peter, whose health appears to have been robust almost up to the final days of his life. Although he reported a sensation of being poisoned, and refused food from 31 October 1828, he was able to take a three-hour walk to and from church on 3 November; and the following day walked over a mile to attend the first of the eternally enigmatic lessons in counterpoint with Simon Sechter. He was too ill to attend the second lesson on 10 November and although he was by then confined to bed, wrote a last letter to his old friend Franz von Schober on 12 November asking for more books to read. In the following days he even managed to finish correcting the proofs of the second part of *Winterreise*. Death was therefore sudden and unexpected, but in retrospect inevitable. The astonishing revelation of the music which had been written in the last months of his short life was yet to come, as was the treasury of earlier compositions which had been passed over, misplaced or forgotten. So much awaited discovery and proper assessment. The gradual and seemingly grudging manner in which this finally occurred, and the final recognition of his genius, is the subject of this book.

Nothing in his letters, conversations or behaviour in his final year suggests that he anticipated his life would be so suddenly cut short. Everything points to an expectation that the great musical developments he pioneered in the last mature works would finally place him on a pedestal alongside his great mentor, Beethoven. But it was not to be, and the world was left to discover for itself, if it so chose, the riches he left to us, and his true standing in the world of music.

BURIAL AND TRIBUTES

Schubert's first grave at Währing Cemetery

Franz Schubert was buried on 21 November 1828, in the Währing cemetery, close to the grave of Beethoven, as he had wished. In the autumn of 1830 a monument was erected on the grave, with money raised from a memorial concert, in the form of a bronze bust of the composer, bearing the epitaph composed by his good friend, the poet and playwright Franz Grillparzer: *'Die Tonkunst begrub hier einen reichen Besitz, aber noch viel schönere Hoffnungen'* ('The art of music here entombed, a rich possession but even fairer hopes'). The reference to 'even fairer hopes' encapsulated the way Schubert's composing career was then perceived. Grillparzer's words neatly sum up the partial and deficient knowledge which his friends and admirers then had of his works, particularly their unawareness of even the existence of the number of major and unperformed works, many of which had by then been collected together by his devoted brother Ferdinand.

The events in the immediate aftermath of Schubert's death, including many memorial tributes, are recorded in great detail and paint a picture of his admirers mourning the loss of such apparently unfulfilled genius. Numerous obituaries and death notices were written, which repeatedly tell us of the reputation which Schubert had gained up to his untimely death. Schoolfriend and loyal admirer Josef von Spaun wrote an extended tribute in March 1829, in which he praised the output of *lieder*, many of which he knew well. But whilst aware of at least some of the composer's other compositions, he commented: 'For the lack of public performances of Schubert's larger works his friends were compensated by his uninterrupted composition of German songs ... .' Von Spaun sadly predicted that 'for the great masses who are but fleetingly entertained by music but not touched or elevated, the Schubert songs will never have more than a small attraction.' Friend and playwright Eduard von Bauernfeld, partly drawing on Spaun's essay, observed that, 'Whether the available larger compositions by Schubert are to be called excellent the future will show ... . However ... what we possess in perfection, that wherein Schubert shows himself unique and unsurpassed – his songs – is alone sufficient to confirm and maintain their creator's fame.'

Another tribute composed shortly after the death was written for the Philharmonic Society by Leopold von Sonnleithner, an avid supporter and friend of many years, who wrote of his 'creative genius that ... could furnish the most carefully thought-out and deeply felt compositions with incredible rapidity.' His then known works were listed as including some 200 songs in print and a similar number in manuscript, together with works in many other categories, including symphonies, masses and 12 completed and four unfinished operas. Recognising that few of the latter had ever been performed on stage, the article added that 'The revival of a German operatic organisation gives rise to the hope they will not much longer be withheld from the public.' Thus can be seen the beginnings of many different perceptions of the composer's status which were to hold sway in the coming years, modified from time to time by the emergence of works unknown till then, but always united by appreciation of the true genius of the man and love for his compositions.

VIENNA

The short span of Schubert's active composing life overlapped with that of many other composers, many of whom visited Vienna as the great centre of European music. Indeed Vienna's reputation in the early years of the nineteenth century could be attributed to the recent presence of Gluck and Mozart, who had died respectively in 1787 and 1791, and even more immediately to that of Haydn and Beethoven. Joseph Haydn resided in the city after his return from London in 1795 and continued composing up until a few years before his death in 1809 – including his final string quartets, and increasingly music for the church. Beethoven had taken up residence in 1792 and was without question the dominant musical influence in Vienna throughout Schubert's life. Although his senior by 27 years, the great man was to die in 1827 when Schubert had just 20 months of his own much shorter life remaining.

Franz was born just over five years after Mozart's death and at a time when the 27-year-old Beethoven was embarking on a career which would seemingly eclipse that of any other composer of that time. These included Joseph Haydn who, when Franz entered the world, had already composed more than 100 symphonies, had completed two extended trips to London and was still active in Vienna. These three Viennese near-contemporaries would be the staple diet of the young Schubert as his musical career developed, such that he would have to stand comparison with their achievements and, with regard to

Beethoven, endure ill-informed and still unfavourable comparison to this day.

The old city of Vienna was, throughout Schubert's lifetime, still surrounded by the defensive walls and an open area known as the *glacis* – designed to repel attackers by exposing them to the defenders' missiles – all of which had stood for several centuries. Indeed these defences had served their purpose well and had helped to repel the Ottoman siege of the city in 1683, a fact not lost on the population nor on theatre audiences, certainly those of Mozart's day. But by the nineteenth century the walls were of no use in military terms. They had entirely failed to deter Napoleon in 1805 and again in 1809. During Schubert's lifetime the *glacis* was progressively built over and both he and Beethoven would be buried in a graveyard in the new district of Währing, located outside the old city. But the walls would not finally be removed until the 1860s when they were replaced by the present *Ringstrasse*, a case of Vienna belatedly catching up with the world. While the old city had been host to Haydn and Beethoven, the new city would become the haunt of Brahms, Strauss (all of them), Mahler, and finally of the second Viennese school. Yet ingrained into its fabric there has remained, for the last two centuries, the shadow and the spirit of perhaps the greatest of its own sons, Franz Schubert, whose true achievements and just reputation would have to wait for nearly a century after his death before they would be properly recognised by the rest of the world, and even by Vienna itself.

BEYOND VIENNA

Franz Seraphicus Peter Schubert was born and spent the whole of his short life living in or within a coach ride of the old city of Vienna. Travels in his twenties took him west as far as Salzburg and east to just beyond the border into Hungary, but no further. He never saw the sea, which figured in many *lieder* but otherwise only in his imagination. Unlike his illustrious contemporaries, he had no opportunity to visit other great capitals of Europe, such as Rome, Paris or London. Yet he lived through two occupations by the French Army, and in 1815 saw all the great European powers assembled in Vienna to settle the future shape of Europe after Napoleon.

Schubert's superlative musical gifts were accompanied by a rather mediocre and even naïve business talent. He seemed unconcerned, initially, with having his music published; the task of getting his compositions printed and into circulation being taken out of his hands by enthusiastic admirers. Even when he had built up an impressive catalogue of published works, he was still forced to haggle in a way that today seems outrageous. His dealings with mercenary publishers usually resulted in him being beaten down to accept shamefully low fees.

Despite this lack of business acumen, he built a modest following in Vienna but sadly failed in various attempts to spread his reputation beyond Austria, with only a very few exceptions. In the eighteenth and early nineteenth centuries, despite the physical constraints on most forms of transport, those who could travel had no great difficulty crossing borders and taking up residence wherever it suited them, money being the only real constraint. So it was that Handel, Haydn, Mozart, Rossini and many other musicians spent long periods on tour and were able to spread their reputation and settle where they were most appreciated. In Handel's case, this was London. For Schubert, journeys outside Vienna were restricted to short trips, to Hungary courtesy of the Esterházy family, and to rural Austria for musical holidays, mostly in the company of Johann Michael Vogl. His lack of travel was the result partly of the repressive regime in Austria in the 1820s, but mainly the absence of fast and cheap transport prior to the railway age.

SCHUBERT'S MUSIC

Today we are inundated with the world's great music, readily available through so many sources at the touch of a screen. Anyone can, therefore, quickly and easily assess which of the composers from the Viennese world of two centuries ago remain favourites with the world's media audiences. The result, whether via radio or any other media platform, is that no programme of 'classical' music can omit Schubert's works, which continue to figure at or near the top of any chart or ranking. That could be because so much of his chamber music seems to fall into neat packages which can brighten the dullest day. But many of the top-ranked pieces we regularly hear are from his great works, such as the String Quintet, the *Trout* Quintet and the piano works, especially the Impromptus. What other composer could claim that his (or her) greatest works were also the most popular? Schubert's music is not only the choice of the connoisseur, it also has a great and lasting appeal to those whose knowledge and appreciation may be superficial but who 'know what they like.' Schubert appeals to all tastes and is to be enjoyed at many levels. But this was not always so. As will be seen, his all too brief span of life ended as it had begun, in relative obscurity. This book will seek to follow the story of how the man and his music came through this hiatus to emerge alongside, and in many ways ahead of, his great contemporaries.

But how was it that the music did not, during Schubert's lifetime, have the effect it has today? The answer to that question will emerge in the course of this book, but in essence it was due to the lack of public awareness coupled, to an extent, with the fickle habits of the Viennese public who had grown used to sensation after the emergence of Mozart and then Beethoven and Rossini. Schubert, unlike his great predecessors, was not a showman. And during the whole course of Schubert's life in Vienna only one public concert dedicated to his music alone was ever put on – and that in the final year of his life.

It is tempting to speculate on how Schubert's career (let alone his compositions) might have developed had he had the opportunity and the inclination to travel outside the restricted sphere in which he spent his life. However, this book will concentrate on what he did in his short life, and how the gradual spread of his music and reputation took place after his early death, as well as introduce the principal characters involved in that process. It will explore how a relatively unknown and obscure composer of *lieder*, from one corner of the huge Austro-Hungarian Empire of the early nineteenth century, has become one of the most celebrated of European composers; one whose music is today familiar throughout the world, and whose works are performed every day of the year and listened to in sold-out concerts by large and enthusiastic audiences. The contrast between the grudging condescension of Schubert's publishers and the reception of his music in the concert halls of the twenty-first century is indeed remarkable and calls for explanation. First and foremost, of course, the spread of Schubert's music and reputation is the natural consequence of the compelling beauty of the music itself.

Schubert's works, as they were known even by the middle of the nineteenth century, and the fluency with which those works were reported to have flowed from his pen, gave rise to a serious belief that, as an untutored rustic, he must have been in receipt of divine inspiration, seemingly taking down music as dictated by the muses. Any acquaintance with the details of his life (which for much of the nineteenth century remained obscure) entirely dispels any such notion, but that was yet another part of the explanation for the Viennese public's reluctance to accept the genius they had in their midst. We therefore now return to the composer's short life and the events leading up to 19 November 1828.

CHAPTER 2
A SHORT LIFE

While Schubert's life is a matter of great interest to musicologists and anyone researching his music, it was a life rendered precious only by the music he created during that sadly brief span. His family was in no way remarkable though most of its members were musically accomplished, which was certainly not unique at the end of the eighteenth century in Vienna. The family led a respectable lower-middle-class existence on the outskirts of the capital city of a great Empire which would survive for just over another century.

THE SCHUBERT FAMILY

Franz Schubert was born into a large family in the rural suburb of Himmelpfortgrund, to the north west of the old city of Vienna, then still surrounded by outmoded defensive walls. Unremarkably for the time, he was the twelfth child of the family, from the marriage of his schoolteacher father, also Franz, to Elisabeth née Vietz. Of the 14 children of the marriage, only five survived. At the time of Franz's birth in 1797 the eldest was Ignaz, 11, who was followed by Ferdinand, aged three, and Karl, aged one. The surviving sister was Maria Theresia, born when Franz was four.

Their mother was to die in 1812, after which father Franz remarried in 1813. The second marriage added two stepsisters, Maria in 1814 (who was to help in nursing Franz during his final illness) and Josepha, born in 1815. While the family was in somewhat lowly circumstances, with no obvious artistic tradition, there was a strong musical current, which meant that Franz would be taught piano at an early age by brothers Ignaz and Ferdinand, and violin by his father. The whole family would regularly perform together, giving the young Franz a ready-made platform for experimenting with string quartets and other combinations of instruments.

Lichtenthal Parish Church

When Franz was just four, the family moved to a rather larger residence almost across the road in the same suburb. Close by and down a long flight of steps, which is still in regular use, lies the local parish church of Lichtental, where the organist and choirmaster, Michael Holzer, soon became aware of and took a special interest in the obvious musical talents of the young Franz, both as a singer and instrumentalist.

At the age of eight, in 1805, he was selected by the court composer Antonio Salieri as a singer for the court chapel; and this was followed by free admission to the Imperial and Royal Seminary, where he was to remain until 1813. There, contrary to popular belief during most of the nineteenth century, he received probably the best musical education that was to be had at that time. This included regular performances and concerts which introduced young Franz to the great music of the day in what was without doubt the world's musical capital. His early compositions, which date from 1810, included a first attempt at an opera. From the outset he regularly made settings of poems discovered through his extensive reading. With his orchestral experience, he was soon able to compose in full orchestral score, a reflection of his thorough musical training and his ability to absorb the music which surrounded him at the seminary.

COMPOSITION LESSONS

In the following year, 1811, Franz's increasingly apparent and prodigious talents led to his being chosen at the age of 14 to attend twice-weekly composition lessons with the celebrated Salieri. This was a privilege he shared with others, including, somewhat later, the young Franz Liszt. The experience led to a burst of further compositions which were tried out on his now admiring schoolfriends. While Salieri encouraged the study of opera scores, especially Italian ones, Franz pursued his own course and in October 1813 completed his First Symphony, for performance by the seminary orchestra. Many commentators have played down the importance of Salieri's tuition but in her recent biography, Lorraine Byrne Bodley* has analysed the documentary record, concluding that this was an important element

---

* *Schubert: A Musical Wayfarer*, 2023.

of the young composer's development. But despite his growing musical talent, and after five years spent at the seminary, family pressures compelled him to return to complete his training as a schoolmaster, and for that purpose to return to live at the family home. Still in the same suburb of Himmelpfortgrund, the family and the school now occupied relatively spacious quarters and so, after a few more months of teacher training, Franz graduated, in August 1814, to become a teaching assistant at his father's school, which by then was prospering. Alongside his conventional career, he was now composing regularly and producing *lieder* at a pace which defies belief.

FIRST ACCLAIM

The parallel career as a composer continued with his first Mass in F, for orchestra, choir, organ and soloists. This was first performed in October 1814, in the same church at Lichtental where Franz had been a choirboy, the particular occasion being the centenary of the church's foundation. The performance, directed by the 17-year-old composer and with Salieri himself present in the congregation, was received with general acclaim. It was given a second performance shortly afterwards by popular demand. In parallel with this achievement, the numbers of *lieder* continued to grow, now approaching 100, including one of his early great compositions, *Gretchen am Spinnrade*, a song which to this day evokes wondrous admiration. In the following year, 1815, often referred to as the *annus mirabilis*, while still pursuing the day job as teaching assistant, he composed 145 *lieder*, including *Erlkönig*, a masterly composition which quickly caught on and has remained a favourite, plus two further symphonies. In 1816, over 100 *lieder* appeared together with two more symphonies, the latest of these being the ever-popular Symphony No 5.

Franz von Schober

After almost two frustrating years of teaching while composing at a bewildering rate, in the autumn of 1816 the 19-year-old Schubert took the momentous decision to leave his teaching post and take up composing as a profession. He left the family home and moved into lodgings in one of the recently developed southern suburbs of the city with a new companion, Franz von Schober, who was to remain a strong influence for the rest of his days. Although the move proved to be a temporary arrangement, from this point onwards his life was devoted to music, living either back at the family home or in various lodgings throughout the city. He managed to eke out a living from composing and, in fact, became the first composer in history to do so without a parallel career as a performer, or the support of a rich benefactor.

LIFE AS A COMPOSER

Life away from his close family was never going to be easy or comfortable. Franz Schubert was below average height and, fortunately for him and for us, was rejected for military service on that account. He had a round, fat face, short neck, not very high forehead, thick brown naturally curly hair, grey-blue eyes, bushy eyebrows, stubby nose and broad, thick lips. He could be taken for a Bavarian peasant, save that he always wore glasses. He was said to become animated when engaged in interesting conversation, especially concerning music, but was otherwise shy, especially in smart society which he encountered only when accompanying his songs. He was indifferent to praise or applause and shunned compliments.* In short, he was not a social animal and took very few steps to promote his music in society.

Once away from the family home and free of interruptions, he composed, during 1817, a large body of piano compositions, 60 *lieder* – including the well-known *Der Tod und das Mädchen* and *Die Forelle* – and orchestral overtures. The bohemian lifestyle, which would become fashionable in opera and drama later in the century was, in reality, a struggle against prejudice and apathy, and the dead hand of commercial publishing. His life was, however, relieved and greatly enriched by the support and devotion of an increasingly wide and lively circle of friends, some with genuine artistic talent in their own right; and by a number of well-to-do admirers, who were to play an important part in the remainder of his career.

Of all Schubert's supporters, none was to have more influence than the recently retired but still active opera singer Johann Michael Vogl. Schubert had heard Vogl on the stage during his schooldays and when introduced to him in 1817, both parties

---

* Leopold von Sonnleithner in O. Deutsch, *Schubert: Memoirs by his Friends*, p 121.

feigned reluctance – Schubert through natural reticence and Vogl through having heard of so many young geniuses who always disappointed. Not this time, however, and as Vogl discovered the true depth of Schubert's genius, their friendship and collaboration grew, spawning the famous series of salon concerts which became known as Schubertiads, a tradition that continues today. Vogl performed the *lieder* almost as they were composed, along with those that had become favourites with the increasingly enthusiastic audiences, which now often included a sprinkling of minor Viennese aristocracy. Schubertiads were held in many of the leading artistic households of Vienna and during travels in a number of provincial towns.

Johann Michael Vogl. Lithograph by Josef Kriehuber

SCHUBERT'S TRAVELS

After the decision to strike out on his own and renounce further teaching, Schubert was soon forced to consider other means of making a living. So when, in 1818, he received an offer from Count Esterházy to accompany his family to their castle at Zseliz in Hungary, to tutor the Count's children and perform at musical soirées, he took up the offer with little hesitation. The autumn months of 1818 were therefore spent with the family, although on this occasion he was accommodated with the servants and retainers. While the Esterházy family were amateur musicians, Schubert also became acquainted at Zseliz with the more talented and influential Baron von Schönstein, who became an important admirer and supporter, and the next most important performer of Schubert's *lieder* after Vogl. It was to Schönstein that Schubert was to dedicate *Die schöne Müllerin*.

On his return to Vienna, music lessons continued, at the Esterházy townhouse in the Herrengasse, thus providing some modest income, and Baron von Schönstein became a regular host and performer of the *lieder*. Some years later, in May 1824, Schubert was induced, again by financial hardship, to accept an offer to make another extended visit to the Esterházy estate, but this time his growing celebrity was recognised by payment of a proper fee and by being accommodated with the family and not with the servants as before. It was on this visit that he is said to have fallen in love with the Count's daughter, Karoline von Esterházy, now 15, and to whom he later, perhaps jokingly, claimed to have dedicated all his compositions. He did dedicate to her his great and celebrated F Minor Fantasia for piano duet, D940, written in the last year of his life. It is tempting to think that the piano scoring – requiring the two performers to cross their hands while performing the music – was an attempt to bring Franz and Karoline closer together; but this was the full extent of the intimacy between the two.

Schubert's collaboration with Vogl led to extended tours, largely at Vogl's expense; the first in the summer of 1819 to Vogl's home town of Steyr in Upper Austria. It was on this tour that Schubert met Sylvester Paumgartner, an enthusiastic amateur who presciently commissioned the celebrated Piano Quintet which became known as *The Trout*. This five-movement piece for piano and string quartet, now including a double bass, incorporated an extra movement with variations on the popular song *Die Forelle (The Trout)*. The work remains one of Schubert's happiest and most popular chamber works – unsurprisingly as the invariable reaction to the music is simply to smile! The tour also took in Linz, where he met old friends from the Stadtkonvikt, including the von Spaun family, and made much music. There were other trips with Vogl in 1823 and an extended tour of over four months in 1825 during which, in addition to visiting Salzburg, it is now accepted he composed the *Great* C Major Symphony, or the majority of it, at Gastein.

SCHUBERT'S LADIES

Supporters and admirers during Schubert's brief life included several highly talented ladies with whom there were some serious, and more casual, attachments (including the aforementioned Karoline), which certainly cast into question theories about his unique preference for men. At the age of 17 he had reportedly fallen in love with Therese Grob, the talented soprano who was just a year younger than Franz, who had taken the solo part in performances of his first mass in 1814.

The relationship continued and blossomed at least up to 1816, when Schubert presented her with a number of manuscript *lieder*, which she kept until her own death. However, in 1820 she married a well-to-do baker in the same Lichtental Church that had seen the start of their relationship. Schubert confessed to have considered marriage with Therese, but at no time would his financial situation have allowed this. Marriage to Karoline von Esterházy was, of course, out of the question, for social reasons in addition to financial ones. Other admirers included Anna Milder, a talented singer, and Anna Fröhlich, pianist and singer, whose friendship was fully reciprocated. It was Anna Fröhlich who organised and performed in the concert given shortly after Schubert's death, which raised the money for his memorial.

A TURNING POINT

A portrait by Leopold Kupelwieser, dated by Schubert himself

The year 1821 can be seen as a pivotal point in Schubert's composing career. The works up until now had included masterpieces by any measure, but from this point Schubert's compositions began to take on the maturity which can be seen as preparing the way for the great achievements of the last years. To some modern writers Schubert had at this stage 'caught up' with his great forbears and contemporaries Mozart and Beethoven, and was writing music which bore its own authority and was no longer under the influence of others. None of this was apparent at the time, especially to the Viennese public which, with the exception of his immediate circle of devoted friends and admirers, remained interested only in the more popular *lieder* and the lighter compositions, including an increasing volume of dances and part songs.

Schubert composed the symphony known as No 7 shortly

after the above portrait was done, probably at Atzenbrugg Castle where other well-known paintings by Kupelwieser were executed. The symphony was written out in orchestral score but with most of the music indicated only as a single line. Other great musical works from 1821 and 1822 included the quartet movement known as the *Quartettsatz* for which Schubert started work on an andante which was left unfinished (perhaps because of the difficulty of creating a fitting continuation); the cantata *Lazarus*; and then the so-called *Unfinished* Symphony, all works of startling originality. But the *Unfinished* Symphony was to have the strangest introduction into the world. In 1823, Schubert was notified that the Styrian Musical Society wished to bestow on him the title of honorary member. No doubt wishing to reciprocate in suitable fashion, Schubert decided to send to the society the incomplete manuscript of the symphony which, by this time, he must have abandoned any intention to complete. He decided to dispatch the work to Graz and for this purpose handed the manuscript, in its incomplete state, to his friend Josef Hüttenbrenner who happened to be travelling to Graz. After this nothing further was heard of its existence until the 1860s when it emerged in the possession of Josef's brother Anselm Hüttenbrenner, as appears later in this narrative.

The *Quartettsatz* was Schubert's twelfth quartet; the earlier works being written for home consumption. Although having only one completed movement, the work represented, as did the *Unfinished* Symphony, the breaking of new and original ground, and formed a significant step towards the composer's final maturity. The *Quartettsatz* was to be followed in 1824 by the great Quartets in A Minor and in D Minor, both of which included movements based on earlier compositions – respectively the theme from the *Rosamunde* ballet music and the song *Death and the Maiden*. The last String Quartet, in G, was composed in 1826 forming a full cycle of quartets spanning what can now be called his early, mature and late period; and these works were to be followed by the incomparable String Quintet in the last months of his life.

PUBLICATION

Schubert had little success in getting his works published and thereby bringing his name and works before a wider public than the circle of admirers in Vienna. Difficulties continued throughout his life in dealing with publishers, who were concerned with ready sales potential rather than artistic merit or integrity. The correspondence with publishers throughout his mature composing life brings to mind the pathetically undignified letters of Mozart to his supposed patrons, who were similarly ineffective in producing the requested support. In Schubert's case, a memorable exchange of correspondence concerned publication of the E flat Trio in 1828, for which the modest sum of 100 florins was asked, only to be beaten down to 60. Schubert's problem, by contrast with Mozart and Beethoven, was that he was not a virtuoso performer; and while his talents spoke loudly to the initiated, the Viennese public were as fickle as those in any other city or any other age in flocking to support the latest celebrity.

In Schubert's case this meant competing for attention with Rossini in the field of operas, and with Paganini in the field of instrumental performances. So, while Schubert's compositions were becoming well known in more refined musical circles, none were published until 1821,* and then only on the initiative of influential friends. The first published works were, unsurprisingly, a group of *lieder* including such masterpieces as *Gretchen am Spinnrade*, *Erlkönig*, *Der Wanderer* and *Morgenlied*. The Deutsch numbers, which reveal the order in which the compositions appeared, show that these works span a significant slice of

---

* The sole exception was *Erlafsee*, a setting of a Mayrhofer poem published as part of an almanac in 1818.

Schubert's composing career, being written between the years 1815 and 1820. Perhaps that would have been insignificant but for the fact that by 1821 he had less than eight years to live.

The publications of 1821 and 1822 seemingly broke a dam, and others followed quickly, practically all of which had been performed mostly in private salon concerts, but were by then well-known, at least to the initiates. These compositions extended up to Opus 14 and consisted of solo and part songs with piano, but with the notable exception of Opus 9 – dances for solo piano – and Opus 10 – piano duets. It will be evident that the opus numbers, which were assigned by the publisher, reveal only the order of publication. It would be well into the next century before the order of composition could be appreciated by the Deutsch numbers assigned to each of the works. Publications in the following year, 1823, commenced with the brilliant *Wanderer* Fantasia for solo piano as Opus 15, and continued with solo and part songs with piano accompaniment and a further set of dances. By this stage, although the publishers were still carefully eyeing the market to assess what was saleable, publications were catching up with the composer's output. Thus, those of 1824 included the first great song cycle *Die schöne Müllerin*, written the previous year and given the Opus number 25, followed by the first of the chamber works to be published, the Quartet in A Minor, written in the year of its publication.

PERFORMANCES

Earlier in his career Schubert had played the viola in an enthusiastic amateur orchestra which met regularly to perform the classics of the time. In 1862, Leopold von Sonnleithner wrote a detailed account of the orchestra and its players, which included a few professionals.* He also noted the music performed which,

---

* See O Deutsch, *Schubert: Memoirs by his Friends*.

in addition to the then standard repertoire (including Handel's *Messiah*), included Schubert's Symphony in B flat (No 5) and 'a larger one in C Major' (No 6) as well as an overture *Im italienischen Stile* (there are two such overtures, D590 and 591). Other works performed included the now lost cantata *Prometheus*. The orchestra was disbanded in 1820 when the premises in which it performed ceased to be available. But performances of Schubert's vocal music, both *lieder* and works for larger groups, continued in different locations, including the Sonnleithner family residence. Leopold, who was a contemporary of Schubert, collected and copied the *lieder* and claimed that many received their first performance at his home 'before a larger circle.'

ILLNESS AND TREATMENT

At some point in 1823 Schubert became aware that he had contracted syphilis, a potentially devastating disease for which there was treatment but no cure, and which would eventually contribute to ending his life prematurely. This inevitably tells us something of the lifestyle he led, seemingly influenced by the company he kept, of which Franz von Schober was a leading light. As a result of the diagnosis he endured a major round of degrading hospital treatments and faced the likelihood of more to follow. Over the next five years, the disease caused discomfort and a level of anxiety that can hardly be imagined, given that Schubert by then must have been well aware of his own abilities and, increasingly, of his rightful place in the contemporary musical world. It remains a matter of speculation how and to what degree this affected his compositions. Superficially, one might regard his earlier works as characteristic of a happier and carefree existence and the later works as bearing the mark of a terrible anxiety. Yet the works themselves hardly bear out any such analysis. Perhaps it is nearer to the truth to think that Schubert retained at least some of his youthful optimism and managed to rise above this terrible affliction through his music.

MUSIC FOR THE THEATRE

Publications and allotment of opus numbers continued up to the first published Piano Sonata, in A Minor, in 1826 as Opus 42. Opus numbers were also allotted by publishers as they worked through the backlog of *lieder* and works for piano solo and duet. These included occasional larger compositions such as the Sonata in G – Opus 78. This great work was renamed by the publisher *Fantasy*, believing that the title 'Sonata' would no longer help to sell the work. An exception to the now regular flow of compositions and publications was the music written for the theatre which required public performance; and here the failure to secure an audience was more acute. Some earlier pieces were performed including the commissioned *Singspiel Die Zwillingsbrüder (The Twins)* in which Vogl had taken the parts of both twins in 1820; and the melodrama *Die Zauberharfe*, performed in the same year. But there were no substantial runs and the few performances were soon forgotten. Despite the lack of success, Schubert remained convinced that the path to recognition – which had so far eluded him – lay through opera. So in the following year he completed a full-length opera, *Alfonso und Estrella*, and in 1823 another, *Fierrabras*. Neither would be performed in his lifetime.

There was hardly better fortune with the play *Rosamunde*, for which he provided incidental music (still widely enjoyed today) and which was played initially to a favourable reception in 1823, but again with few performances and no further recognition. During the remaining years of his life, Schubert continued to work at what were to be grand operas, the last of these being *Der Graf von Gleichen* (1827), composed to a libretto by his friend, the playwright Eduard von Bauernfeld. But none were completed or performed, and the manuscripts from all his endeavours were left with the host of other unknown works at his death. Other major compositions of 1827 were the Piano Trio in E flat and the celebrated song cycle *Winterreise*. The Piano Trio in B flat, often attributed to 1827 was, in the view of many, composed some two years earlier. Composition of further *lieder* and shorter piano compositions continued – these being the works demanded by the publishers, who remained less interested in the major works. Beethoven died in March 1827, with Schubert being one of the mourners at the funeral. In September of that year he spent a short holiday in Graz with Johann Baptist Jenger, pianist and member of the local music society, meeting up with other old friends including Anselm Hüttenbrenner: the last excursion Schubert was to enjoy.

A FIRST SCHUBERT CONCERT

Despite all this activity, by the beginning of 1828 no single orchestral work had been published. There were by now nine symphonies, seven masses (with another to be composed in the final year) and a huge array of chamber music, most of which had been performed on just a few occasions and in private salons. Early in the year friends and supporters decided something had to be done to promote Schubert's reputation in Vienna and set about organising a public concert. This was finally held at the Musikverein premises on 27 March 1828, the first anniversary of Beethoven's death. The works performed, consisting entirely of Schubert's music, were the first movement of a new quartet (the G Major), *lieder* sung by Vogl: *Der Kreuzzug, Die Sterne, Fischerweise* and *Fragment aus dem 'Aeschylus;' Ständchen* sung by Josefine Fröhlich, a piano trio (the E flat) performed by Messrs Bocklet, Bohm and Linke, *Auf dem Strom* with piano and horn, *Die Allmacht* sung by Vogl, and *Schlachtgesang* for male chorus. Seven of the works given (six of the *lieder* and the movement of the Quartet in G) were receiving their first public performances. This was the first such concert and it was to be the last. Of the two chamber works played, neither would be heard again for some years, and in the case of the quartet, the first full performance had to wait until the 1850s. The audience in March 1828 was full of enthusiasm and the concert made a good profit, which fortunately went to the composer. But it was only through the recollections of friends that the event was recorded. It was all but ignored by the press, who were busy reviewing a recital by Paganini.

THE FINAL YEAR

We have now reached 1828, the last year of Schubert's life, in which his compositions apparently began with the composing of, or at least the final editing of, the *Great* C Major Symphony. Modern scholarship has now revealed that, in all probability, this was no more than redating, by Schubert, of the manuscript of the work that had been completed much earlier. However, the final year was to witness an astonishing host of major new compositions which must now be seen as the final flowering of his genius. The F Minor Fantasia for piano duet, as we have seen, was dedicated to Caroline Esterházy. *Lieder* of that year, including his startling Heine and Rellstab settings, were to be collected together as the *Schwanengesang* cycle (the name being the invention of the publisher, Haslinger, although not inappropriate). Compositions continued with the last three great piano sonatas, the incomparable String Quintet, and the sixth and last Mass in E flat, which embodies highly original and forward-looking choral and orchestral music. The three piano sonatas are, today, often played as a set in their apparent order of composition – C Minor, A Major and B flat – giving the impression that the first two are in some way leading up to the final climax in the third. But it seems likely that the three, together with the String Quintet, were composed at the same time, such is the inter-relationship of the music; and all these pieces stand equally as the final outpouring of his genius. Sometime during the year he sketched out a new symphony in D, quite different to the *Great* C Major, which would have been taken up and completed had he lived.

POSTHUMOUS PUBLICATIONS

Franz Schubert died on 19 November 1828. At the time of his death publications had reached Opus 100 (the Trio in E flat). The B flat Trio had already been allotted Opus 99, but did not appear until 1836; and there were many more works in course of publication in November 1828. To this backlog had to be added the works passed to the publisher Diabelli in early 1829 so that publications and allotment of opus numbers of songs and other compositions would continue for many years. Among the works held back by the publishers was the second set of four Impromptus, finally published in 1839 as Opus 142, and now one of the most popular of the solo piano works. The great G Major Quartet was published only in 1851 as Opus 161 and the String Quintet in 1853 as Opus 163. The Octet, which had been performed at the time of its composition in 1824, was published only in 1853, as Opus 166. Publications and further opus numbers continued up to the last batch of songs – which still included some relatively early ones – being published as Opus 173 nos 1-6 in 1876. Thus, for nearly half a century after his death, Schubert's works continued to appear as though the composer was still at work. Sadly this was not so and his memory would fade as new composers appeared on the scene both in Vienna and throughout Europe. But we shall now examine how the memory and true stature of this great composer has been gradually brought to life during the two centuries since his death.

CHAPTER 3
THE AFTERMATH

The funeral took place on 21 November 1828, in bad weather but with a large attendance. The coffin was carried by young officials and students to St Josef's Church, Margareten, where a chorus accompanied by wind instruments performed Schubert's *Pax vobiscum* to a new text composed by von Schober at the family's request. After a blessing, the coffin was carried to the church of St Lorenz and St Gertrud at Währing, where a second ceremony followed with the singing of the *Miserere* and *Libera me*. It was then conveyed to the new Währing cemetery, where it was interred as close as possible to the grave of Beethoven, as Schubert had wished, with only three more recent graves separating the two.

MEMORIALS AND TRIBUTES

A memorial service, organised by Schubert's friend and supporter Josef Hüttenbrenner, was held on 23 December 1828 at the rather grander court church of St Augustine near the Burg. Invitations were circulated with an appeal for contributions towards a gravestone. The music performed was the *Requiem for Double Chorus* by Josef's brother Anselm. The music was not well received, according to a report in the Leipzig newspaper the *Allgemeine Musikalische Zeitung*. It was unclear at that time why one of Schubert's many masses was not performed (the true interests of the Hüttenbrenner brothers would not emerge for another three decades).

On 30 January 1829, a day short of what would have been Schubert's 32nd birthday, a private memorial concert, organised by Schubert's friend and admirer Anna Fröhlich, was held at the chancellery of the Philharmonic Society. This was both a celebration of Schubert's life and an opportunity to raise funds for a monument to be erected at the grave. The concert included a number of Schubert's *lieder* together with a piano trio, almost certainly the E flat Trio, which had also been given at the public concert organised in March 1828, and performed by the same trio led by Karl Bocklet. The event was concluded by a performance of the first finale from Mozart's *Don Giovanni*. The concert was well supported and successful in raising sufficient funds for a bust of Schubert to be commissioned from the sculptor Josef Alois Dialer, which was subsequently installed on the grave at Währing.

LIFE AFTER SCHUBERT

Once the funeral and memorial events were concluded, Schubert's friends and admirers had to become accustomed to a life without their friend and hero. There was never any question of Schubert being forgotten. Letters were exchanged between his friends in the weeks and months following the death which record musical parties in which many of the *lieder* were sung. Anton Ottenwalt, poet and Schubert supporter, recorded on 8 February 1829 such a musical event the previous evening, noting that the music 'had, in a strange way, taken hold of us all.'

Schubert's loyal friend Josef von Spaun, who was invited to contribute to a much later collection of memoirs by Ferdinand Luib in 1858, recalled that the sad loss of Schubert did not prevent our enjoying his creations, rather did it stimulate us in this respect; at my house and especially at that of my hospitable friend Hofrat Witteczek, Vogl and Schönstein, accompanied by Mikschlik or Jenger, sang the glorious songs, which called forth increasing enthusiasm. Anyone who has heard Vogl sing *Winterreise* ... has something to take with him throughout his whole life and will never hear anything more beautiful.*

Josef von Spaun

Vogl had, of course, performed most of the *lieder* with Schubert himself and continued to perform after the death. Though some 30 years older than Schubert and now of advancing years, he remained devoted to the music, particularly to *Winterreise*, of which he gave a complete performance shortly before his own death in 1840. This happened to fall on 19 November, the twelfth anniversary of Schubert's own death.

The Rellstab and Heine settings of 1828 (D957), which had

---

* Deutsch, *Schubert: Memoirs by his Friends*.

been acquired by the publisher Haslinger, were smartly published under the now familiar title of *Schwanengesang*, and given their first public performance in Vienna, along with *Mirjams Siegesgesang* (D942) on 30 January 1829. By chance, this was the same evening as the memorial concert at the Philharmonic Society. Strangely, and despite the growing enthusiasm for new *lieder*, Schubert's last song *Der Hirt auf dem Felsen* (D965) did not receive a public performance until March 1830, and then in Riga, but was performed in Vienna shortly afterwards. However, the final and magnificent E flat Mass (D950), completed in July 1828, was performed within a year of the composer's death, at the Alserkirche, on 4 October 1829, with his brother Ferdinand conducting. He also conducted the second performance in the Church of Mariatrost on 15 November 1829.

CONTINUED PERFORMANCES

There are records of public performances of a number of chamber works performed shortly after his death, including the *Wanderer* Fantasia (although it was nearly a decade after publication). On 12 March 1833, the Quartet in D Minor (D810) is recorded as being performed in Berlin, indicating that there must have been earlier performances in Vienna. There were also a number of public concerts at which some of Schubert's orchestral works were heard, most for the first time. It must be remembered that, apart from performances of the masses in Vienna's churches, there had been only one public concert devoted entirely to Schubert's music, which was held on 27 March 1828, and that had included only chamber, *lieder* and choral works. Any public performance of Schubert's orchestral music was therefore a special event, even if posthumous. In the years following his death there were performances, in 1829 of the overture to *Fierrabras*, and in March 1830 a performance conducted by Ferdinand of three orchestral works: the Overture in B flat (D470), the *Kantate zu Ehren von Josef Spendon* (D472), the final chorus from *Fernando* (D220) and the *Overtüre Im Italienischen Stil*. In April 1830, Acts I and II of the unfinished oratorio *Lazarus* (D689) were performed at the Annakirche, Vienna, and in 1833 the oratorio *Stabat Mater* (D383) was given.* These performances were unusual and significant events given the lamentable indifference of the Viennese to Schubert's orchestral music during his lifetime. However, the change of attitude was not to last, and after 1833 a relative silence descended as the world returned to its earlier view of Schubert as a composer of *lieder*. There were no further recorded performances of the orchestral music until the end of the decade, and then not in Vienna but in Leipzig, as a result of the intervention of Robert Schumann.

THE *LIEDER* AND DANCES

While the *lieder* for solo voice and piano represented the medium through which Schubert became known in Vienna, and by which his fame was to spread through Europe both before but especially following his death, he was also celebrated as a prolific composer of dances. Many sets of *Tänze, Ländler, Écossaises* and *Walzer* were published in his lifetime, and it was through these that Schumann first became acquainted with Schubert's works. Their popularity continued after Schubert's death, and contributed to keeping the composer's name alive in his own city. In addition to the solo *lieder*, Schubert also composed many part songs, those for male voices being particularly popular. While part songs have now largely fallen out of fashion, they attracted many enthusiastic amateurs then, particularly in Vienna in the 1820s and 1830s, and have continued their popularity into the twentieth century. There is no doubt that Schubert composed these often charming numbers virtually to order, after playing for dances *extempore* and then writing down those that appealed to him. One of the best attested stories is of the compo-

---

* Janet I Wasserman, *The Schubertian*, April 2009.

of his *Ständchen* ('*Zögernd leise*') to words by Grillparzer (D920) to the specific order of his friend Anna Fröhlich, as a birthday present for a pupil. The wonderful piece was composed in short order but was then found to have been arranged for contralto and male voice chorus, when the request had been for a ladies' chorus! Undaunted, Schubert rapidly rearranged the music for the requested ensemble, now allotted its own designation as D921. The performance on a lovely summer's evening was said to have been unforgettable, although Schubert himself either forgot or did not bother to attend.

The popularity of part songs was reflected in the setting up of a number of amateur choral societies, particularly the Wiener Männergesang-Verein, for male voices, established in 1845, which became a serious force in promoting Schubert's music in the mid-nineteenth century, and which remains active today. The dances likewise remain popular and very much still in the repertory, often appearing today as piano solo insertions in concert programmes, between more substantial piano compositions. However, in the years following the death, with the exception of a number of concerts at which a few of the orchestral works were heard for the first time, the activity soon died down and reverted to a situation much like that in the years before the death, with Schubert known primarily as the composer of *lieder*.

Sadly, the failure of Schubert's music to win a large and popular following in Vienna during his lifetime was soon reflected in a falling off of interest in his works, with the exception of those which had caught the public's approval – the *lieder* and other vocal pieces, especially male-voice part songs. For the rest it would be a matter of waiting and hoping for a better outcome at some time to come.

POPULAR MUSIC IN VIENNA

The problem of promoting the works of the dead composer in his home city was not new. Like any urban population, the good citizens of Vienna were motivated by fashion and tradition and in the 1820s and 1830s the fashion was for dances, increasingly for waltzes, played by small orchestras which could perform in any place where there was an audience. Schubert himself would have been familiar with the ländler and waltzes played in the Café Rebhuhn, and other familiar hostelries, by a small band led by Joseph Lanner. He would also have heard a second band led by Lanner's contemporary and rival Johann Strauss (the First), whose somewhat hackneyed repertoire consisted of a limited number of dances played frequently but with gusto and what became famous as Viennese panache. This was popular music that caught the imagination, not just of Vienna, but eventually of the whole of Europe including England, where the Strauss ensemble was invited to take part in Queen Victoria's coronation celebrations in 1838.

Johann Strauss the First died in 1849 but left a dynasty including Johann the Second, and also Josef and Eduard, all of whom became international celebrities in the continuing craze for authentic Viennese dance music. Eduard fathered another Johann, the Third, who carried the Strauss tradition into the twentieth century. Johann the First was responsible for promoting the winter *Fasching* (carnival), a tradition that still continues. The Viennese did not forget Mozart or Beethoven, and the parallel tradition of serious music later attracted Brahms and Mahler, and eventually the later Richard Strauss. But this was the background against which Schubert and his admirers and promoters had to struggle to make themselves heard above the endless din of cheap entertainment.

CHAPTER 4
FERDINAND SCHUBERT

Ferdinand Schubert, teacher and musician, was to play a pivotal role in promoting his deceased brother's music and reputation. Three years older than Franz, Ferdinand was close to him throughout his life and it was in his family apartment that Franz died. Ferdinand found himself the custodian of the precious hoard of manuscripts left by Franz, and their fate and the future of his brother's reputation were in his hands and no-one else's. Ferdinand was neither well-off nor well-connected and had a large family of his own to support. Yet at the time of Franz's death there was no person in a better position to know and appreciate the true extent of his brother's genius, and the worth of the hoard of manuscripts that had fallen into his charge.

A CLOSE-KNIT FAMILY

Born into the same modest but close-knit family as Franz, Ferdinand followed substantially the same life story that his younger brother would follow. This included being taught violin by his father, piano by elder brother Ignaz, and singing and organ by Michael Holzer at the same Lichtental Parish Church, behind the cramped, communal family apartment. His professional career was primarily as a teacher, as indeed was the pattern later intended for Franz. And like his famous younger brother, Ferdinand also became a serious musician, playing the violin and organ to a professional level and being credited with over 90 compositions, some of which were published.

Ferdinand Schubert in later life

The Schubert family home was filled with music, particularly string quartets, for which the young Franz composed a series of early works, from D2 and 3, followed by D18-20, between 1810 and 1812. Ferdinand was the leader of the quartet with Ignaz as second violin, their father on cello and Franz playing viola. And when not playing at home, Ferdinand and Franz both played in the amateur orchestra which met regularly in the house of Otto Hatwig, professional musician and conductor, where performances included at least two of Franz's symphonies (5 and 6) and one of his Italian overtures.

The brothers were indeed close and their correspondence reveals a genuine and mutual affection which led, in the last stages of Franz's life, to his temporary move to Ferdinand's new apartment in the Neu-Wieden suburb, which also accommodated his wife and their eight children. The apartment, at 6 Kettenbrückengasse, is now a museum, in which visitors can see the small side room in which the composer's final days were spent. What is particularly striking is how the small apartment could have accommodated Ferdinand and his family as well as Franz and his half-sister Maria, who helped to nurse him through his final illness. It is clear that Ferdinand had a deep admiration and love for his brother; but of course it is the service that Ferdinand was to play in the preservation and spread of the music, and reputation of his deceased brother, that is of interest. It was a service that was thrust upon him without warning in November 1828, and which was to be pivotal in ensuring that the genius of his dead brother would eventually be appreciated by the rest of humanity.

FERDINAND'S CAREER

Unlike Franz, Ferdinand completed his teacher training and in 1816 left their father's school, striking out on his own to become a full-time teacher, which was soon supplemented by his appointment as a choirmaster. His organ-playing skills were such that he applied, in 1822, for the post of second court organist, albeit unsuccessfully. However, he continued to play the organ in various churches including the local Lichtental Parish Church. Teaching activities included lessons for piano, organ and violin; and his compositions included songs, choruses and *Singspiele* to be performed by his pupils, as well as more ambitious masses and other sacred works. It is in the context of a number of works of shared authorship with his younger brother that Ferdinand's reputation as a composer has become questionable if not notorious. The fact that the brothers co-operated on a modest number of compositions was not a secret. As will be seen, at the time of the first full biography by Heinrich Kreissle von Hellborn, published in 1865, a catalogue of Franz's compositions included his *Deutsche Trauermesse* (D621) which, while then attributed to Franz, is stated to be *'without doubt a Requiem written by Ferdinand Schubert.'* Such was the belief and indeed reputation of Ferdinand at that time. Subsequent discovery has revealed otherwise.

George Grove, after his first and notable visit to Vienna in 1867, made a second visit in 1880 while working on his biography of Schubert, during which he visited surviving members of the Schubert family including Carola Geisler-Schubert, a descendant of Ferdinand's second wife. From her he obtained and subsequently published a hitherto unknown letter confirming that the particular composition was indeed that of Franz. The letter,* dated 24 August 1818, was written while Schubert was at Zseliz, acting as tutor to the children of the Esterházy family and doubtless bored with being away from Vienna and his friends. The letter reads:

> It is half-past eleven at night, your German Requiem is finished. It made me sad, believe me, for I sang it from the depth of my soul. Add what is missing, ie write in the words below the music and the signs above it. If you wish to make a number of repeats, do so, without writing to Zseliz to ask me about it ... .

Ferdinand completed the work and conducted it in September 1818, as his own composition, and in 1819 used it for an examination, as a result of which he secured an appointment. It was later published by Diabelli in 1826 as a work of Ferdinand.

---

* O Deutsch, *The Schubert Reader: A Life of Franz Schubert in Letters and Documents*, p 94.

Other compositions under the name of Ferdinand have been established as either the work of Franz or based on compositions by Franz, usually through forensic musical analysis rather than direct evidence as for the German Requiem. But on one occasion, in the case of the cantata *Namensfeier für Franz Michael Vierthaler* (D294), Ferdinand himself revealed the true composer in his catalogue of the works of Franz, drawn up as part of the biographical note on Franz Schubert, which he produced in 1839.* The note reveals, surprisingly, that Franz also wrote minuets and trios for their elder brother Ignaz!

BROTHERLY LOVE

So, was Ferdinand a mere plagiarist, intent on gaining as much self-glorification as he could from the reflected genius of his brother? Such a suggestion would be to misunderstand entirely the close relationship between the brothers, which is so clearly revealed in their often intimate correspondence throughout Franz's life. They run from the letter of a hungry schoolboy of 1812 appealing to his elder brother for funds,† to the affectionate letter from Ferdinand addressed to Franz during his triumphant tour of Upper Austria with Vogl in 1825.‡ Their correspondence shows, in Ferdinand's case, a close familiarity with Franz's compositions and their progress in terms of publication and performance. But they also reveal a genuine brotherly love, the closeness of which may be unfamiliar and unusual in the present age.

But it was a love that was entirely consistent with a desire of the elder brother to advance his own musical career, when it was quite apparent to both that Franz's talents far outweighed the modest abilities of Ferdinand. Franz was never possessive about

---

* See Deutsch, *Memoirs by his Friends*, p 36.
† Deutsch, *Docs*, Letter 24 November 1812, No 46.
‡ Deutsch, *Docs*, Letter 4 August 1825, No 577.

his compositions and was content to leave his manuscripts with any of his close friends, and even made copies of favourite songs for them. It should be no surprise that Franz's affection for his brother extended to helping him with compositions which, while they stretched Ferdinand's efforts to the fullest, came so easily and rapidly to the pen of Franz. Equally it should be no surprise that Ferdinand, after his brother's sudden and untimely death, took on the mantle of seeing that his dead brother's works, still waiting to be recognised, were safeguarded, promoted where possible and eventually revealed to the world, including those compositions which Ferdinand knew were not his own.

AFTER THE DEATH

Following the funeral and the memorial concert, Ferdinand, who almost certainly had a better appreciation of his brother's true achievements than any man then alive, was not idle. He, of course, had only a limited appreciation of the activities of 1828, apart from the final weeks when Franz was in residence with the family. But Ferdinand must also have been acutely aware that no other person had knowledge of the scale of Schubert's monumental output. Indeed, most of the friends and admirers would have been aware only of the *lieder* and the few other works they had had the chance to hear. And as well as having perhaps the best appreciation of the true measure of his genius, Ferdinand knew that there existed a vast array of manuscripts that had been left in many different places and in the care of many different admirers, who were now, regrettably, turning into collectors.

Ferdinand knew that no catalogue of the compositions existed. Unlike Mozart and Beethoven, Schubert had kept no list of his works as they were composed other than by frequently endorsing the manuscript with the date (and sometimes the time) of composition. Having recorded the date, he often left his manuscripts wherever they happened to be completed although

Franz did retain a collection of manuscripts which he took with him when moving lodgings. So, on his final move to Ferdinand's apartment he brought with him what was to be the start of the collection which Ferdinand would then proceed to build up in the famous iron chest kept in the apartment. This was to hold the treasures of the lifetime's work of the composer.

Clearly aware of its importance, and aware that no other person would be in a better position to preserve the manuscripts and establish the future reputation of his brother, Ferdinand set about gathering together other manuscripts from wherever they could be found. As the manuscripts were collected, he also set about preparing what would be the first catalogue of the works. Many of the early compositions had been left at their father's schoolhouse in the Grunertorgasse, and many had been copied and collected by his schoolfriends at the seminary. Particular friends were Johann Leopold Ebner and Albert Stadler, each of whom made copies of what they had heard and continued their enthusiasm for Schubert's music after leaving to pursue separate careers; and each of these friends in the 1850s provided valuable notes on Schubert's life. Many of the works of the 1820s were reported to be stored in the music closet in his rooms at von Schober's house in the Tuchlauben. Fortunately, Ferdinand managed to bring together most of these collections, along with the manuscripts which the composer had in his possession, which included the works of the last few months of his life. Ferdinand also set about collecting together the operas, symphonies and masses, which had been left in many different locations, and many other works, all of which went into the iron chest for safekeeping while Ferdinand worked out what to do to secure his brother's reputation for posterity.

SALE OF THE COMPOSITIONS

Ferdinand did not wait long in seeking to arrange publication of the manuscripts wherever he could, with the necessary additional objective of raising some money to pay for the medical treatment in the last weeks of Schubert's life, the cost of which had fallen on him. Franz did not leave a will and while there was uncertainty about his rights in respect of the manuscripts, the family was content to leave Ferdinand to administer the estate and deal with financial affairs. Thus, on 29 November 1828, only 10 days after the composer's death, Ferdinand offered a large quantity of manuscripts comprising all the songs for solo voice and piano, piano music and chamber works to Diabelli & Co (later Spina & Co). On 17 December 1828, Ferdinand also recorded that he had handed over to the publisher Tobias Haslinger the last 13 songs, plus the last three piano sonatas, for a total fee of 500 florins. This sum was swiftly accounted for in defraying the cost of medical treatment in the final days, amounting to 325 florins, and the funeral expenses of 269 florins.

The 13 songs, with the addition of *DieTaubenpost*, were to become the aptly named *Schwanengesang*, which, as noted, was speedily published and performed at the end of January 1829. The offer, which had been made to Diabelli on 29 November 1828, was accepted only in early 1830 and resulted in the publication of the hitherto unpublished songs in 50 instalments, spread out over the next 20 years. It was this understandably cautious approach that led to the popular rumour that Schubert was still alive and still composing *lieder*. Of the manuscripts which Ferdinand collected, he disposed privately of some which appeared unsuitable for publication, including the sketches for the *Unfinished* Symphony. Although apparently sold to Haslinger, the three last sonatas were handed over to Diabelli but not published until 1838. They were then seemingly forgotten for many decades, perhaps as a result of an unfavourable review by Robert Schumannn, published in 1840 and republished in 1850.

ATTEMPTS TO SECURE PERFORMANCES

During the 1830s Ferdinand held positions with Vienna's most prominent musical society, the Gesellschaft der Musikfreunde (also known as the Musikverein), which gave him the opportunity to organise musical events promoting his deceased brother's music. This he did with enthusiasm, employing his own composing skills to arrange Schubert's works for the available instruments, often with piano reductions and other adaptations. Ferdinand also promoted concerts, some of which he conducted himself, including the two performances of the final great Mass in E flat, which took place in October and November 1829. Ferdinand organised other performances in the years following the death, but after 1833 a relative silence descended, with no further performances of Schubert's music planned or likely to take place, in Vienna or elsewhere.

For Ferdinand this must have been a dispiriting experience, seeing his brother's once bright and promising future diminished and replaced, as in earlier days, by a reputation as a composer of German *lieder*, the genre in which Schubert had excelled, but which might also pall as the fickle Viennese public clamoured for the latest musical novelty. And despite Franz's own efforts, there had been little spread of his reputation outside Vienna. Ferdinand thus remained the sole custodian of the chest laden with masterpieces of which the world remained in ignorance. Even the works which had been sold to Diabelli, including many masterpieces of chamber music and orchestral scores, lay unperformed and unheeded on the publisher's shelves, as the public's memory of Franz Schubert faded away.

Then in 1835, over six years after the death, Ferdinand decided to make a further attempt to secure performances, if not publication. At his own expense he placed advertisements in newspapers in Vienna, Leipzig and Paris, in March and April of that year, offering performing rights for a number of operas, symphonies and masses. The advertisements included the following:

> Franz Schubert, the composer of genius and soulful song-writer who departed this life all too soon, has left behind a number of musical works remaining in his brother's hands, which the latter, partly in order not to deprive the world of these works, and partly also to make use for his own benefit of his brother's spiritual heritage according to the deceased's wish, is willing to assign for performance to theatre managements and musicians at moderate fees. These works are I Operas (nine listed). II Symphonies (seven listed). III Masses (five listed).
>
> Whoever desires anything of the above is requested to get into touch with Herr Ferdinand Schubert, Teacher, at the I & R Training School in Vienna.

Despite the apparent attraction of what was offered, no further sales or performances are recorded as resulting from this initiative. However, although he was unaware at the time, Ferdinand had set in motion a chain of events which would, in due course, lead to the precious manuscripts within the iron chest being brought to the attention of the musical world outside Vienna.

The first link in the chain of events was the fact that Ferdinand's advertisement had been seen by Robert Schumann. He had a very limited knowledge of Schubert's compositions other than the dances and piano pieces he had played and appreciated as a student, and the *Wanderer* Fantasia which he had performed. But this was sufficient for him to reprint the advertisement in the *Neue Zeitschrift für Musik*, of which Schumann was then the editor, in Leipzig. Again there was no response to the reprinted advertisement but Schumann remembered the event when, in 1838, he moved to take up temporary residence in Vienna. It was on New Year's Day 1839 that Schumann decided to take a walk, the primary purpose of which was to visit Schubert's grave at Währing cemetery; but he also remembered the advertisement and decided, without any prior announcement, to pay a visit to Ferdinand Schubert who, fortunately, was at home. This led to Schumann examining the contents of the iron chest and, eventually, to the re-emergence of the *Great* C Major Symphony, the involvement of Mendelssohn and a first performance, as will be seen.

THE *GREAT* C MAJOR SYMPHONY

Ferdinand played a vital and early role in the preservation and promotion of this masterpiece. As already seen, the work was composed in 1825 and completed probably in 1826 but, despite suggestions to the contrary, the manuscript was not then sent to the Musikverein to which it was to be presented. An undated letter exists from Franz to the Musikverein which Deutsch suggests was dated early October 1826,[*] and reads as follows:

> To the Committee of the Austrian Musical Society
>
> Convinced of the Austrian Musical Society's noble intention to support any artistic endeavour as far as possible, I venture, as a native artist, to dedicate to them this, my symphony, and to commend it most politely to their protection.
>
> With all respect
>
> Your devoted,
>
> Frz Schubert

Deutsch supposed this to refer to the lost Gastein Symphony

---

[*] Deutsch: *Docs*, No 709.

but that outdated notion can now be confidently discounted. Puzzlingly, the Musikverein records refer to a symphony being dedicated to the society by Schubert in October 1826, and other documents record both the presentation to and receipt by Schubert of the sum of 100 florins in appreciation of the dedication.* But no manuscript from 1826 is known to exist and it is certain there was no 'lost' symphony.

Instead, the Musikverein has in its possession the original manuscript of the *Great* C Major Symphony with Schubert's now well-known amendments. The explanation, although not documented, must be that the symphony was intended for the Musikverein in 1826 and, although promised (and 'paid' for), was held back by Schubert, who intended to make revisions. Those were the changes, in places very significant, which were made by Schubert and were found in the version of the manuscript that was in the possession of the Musikverein when inspected by George Grove in 1867, when he made a careful note of the changes.† What remains unclear is how the manuscript got to the Musikverein bearing its new date, in Schubert's own hand, of March 1828. It is less of a mystery how the symphony came to be sent to Leipzig in 1839. The answer to this question is that Ferdinand had made a copy of the symphony, including Schubert's amendments, and this was the version preserved in the iron chest that would be inspected by Schumann on his visit in 1839. This was also the copy subsequently sent to Leipzig and from which the work was performed and published, while the original manuscript with the alterations remained in Vienna and remains there, bearing the date of March 1828.

It remains uncertain when Ferdinand's copy was made and when the original manuscript, bearing Schubert's changes, was finally presented to the Musikverein. Ferdinand's copy must have been made before the presentation. The Musikverein

---

* Deutsch: *Docs*, Nos 710, 712, 719.
† Appendix to English translation of von Hellborn's *Life of Franz Schubert*, 1869.

planned to perform the new symphony in December 1828 and must have had a copy of the work some time in advance to allow copyists to prepare the orchestral parts. It is known that rehearsals were embarked on and, according to Maurice Brown, it was Schubert himself who, when the work was found to be too difficult, withdrew the symphony and offered the smaller Symphony No 6, which was the work actually performed at the concert. The concert finally took place on 14 December 1828, by which time Schubert was dead. The likely sequence of events was, therefore, that Ferdinand, being aware of the changes his brother had made to the manuscript, took the opportunity to make his own copy of the work, as amended, some time before the original was delivered to the Musikverein. The orchestral parts were probably copied from Ferdinand's fair copy; but if so, this copy was later recovered and retained by Ferdinand and the original manuscript with Schubert's changes was then delivered to the Musikverein.

REDATING THE SYMPHONY

It still remains a mystery why the symphony was annotated with the date of 1828 by Schubert himself. A possible explanation has emerged from further research* inter alia by John Reed, who was the first scholar to assign the correct date of 1825 to the symphony. The research is to the effect that Schubert made the changes to the manuscript, not in March 1828 as would appear from the manuscript, but not later than 1827 and possibly shortly after the original composition. The date of March 1828, it is suggested, was added by Schubert himself to improve the chances of securing publication of what would then appear to be a 'new' work, although in fact now some years old.

If this is the true explanation it tells us something of Schubert's state of mind in the early part of the momentous year of

---

* See Brian Newbould, *Schubert and the Symphony* p 211-212.

1828. For these events surely indicate a composer still concerned at having his music performed, knowing that many of his greatest works had as yet received no public performance. What it does not suggest is a man surrendering to his fate and preparing to compose his own swan song. And whatever the true story of the manuscript copies of the symphony, it is clear that Ferdinand played a central role, and one that was finally to be crowned with success in the symphony's performance. But this was not for another decade, and not in Vienna but in Leipzig.

SCHUMANN'S VISIT

A decade later, Ferdinand was able to produce his fair copy of the symphony for the inspection of Schumann, which would finally lead to a complete performance of the work. It might be said that once Schumann and Mendelssohn became engaged with this, and others of Schubert's works, the emergence of the other masterpieces was inevitable. As will be seen, however, the progress in disseminating the priceless works remained painfully slow and was still in progress at the time of Ferdinand's death in 1859. Furthermore, while Schumann took great interest in the *Great* C Major Symphony and some of the piano works, he showed no interest in the other symphonies, or the masses or the operas. The manuscripts which Ferdinand continued to preserve for a further two decades included all these and many other works, almost without exception in their original manuscript form, and of which no other copies existed. Their continued survival was a tribute to Ferdinand's devotion and appreciation of the treasures with which he found himself charged. And as will be seen, Vienna in the middle years of the nineteenth century was not an entirely peaceful environment. Without Ferdinand's diligence and perseverance there could be no guarantee that the works, including the *Great* C Major Symphony, would ever have been heard.

THE REMAINING MANUSCRIPTS

In addition to the works collected together by Ferdinand shortly after his brother's death, there were many other manuscripts in existence which, as Schubert's celebrity gradually emerged, would become increasingly treasured by their owners or possessors. Notorious among these were the manuscripts in the possession of the Hüttenbrenner brothers, Anselm and Josef, in Graz, which in addition to a sizeable collection of operas, *lieder* and other vocal works, included the then unrecorded and unknown *Unfinished* Symphony, the discovery of which was still some decades away. Also in Graz, the Pachler family, whom Schubert had visited in 1827, held other original scores including the manuscript of *Alfonso und Estrella*. Schubert had left this work with the family in the hope of securing a performance, which never happened.

The opera manuscript lay forgotten in Graz until 1842, when it was handed back to Ferdinand and sent by him to Liszt, who was to arrange its first performance. In Linz both Josef von Spaun and Albert Stadler, former schoolfriends and admirers, possessed a number of *lieder* and piano works, the existence of which was not to be revealed for many years. Karoline Esterházy at Zseliz held a number of manuscripts dating from the two periods in 1818 and 1824 when Schubert was the resident music tutor, including songs and piano and chamber works. Other works were in the possession of numerous friends and colleagues including duplicated versions of popular songs, some with significant variants. These works in private hands largely remained so and in the following decades found their way into other private hands and then generally into museums where they now reside. The gradual reassembly of Schubert's scattered manuscripts was a long affair, which continued for many years, up to the last decades of the nineteenth century.

THE COLLECTORS

Perhaps inevitably, given Schubert's apparent lack of concern for the security of his manuscripts, some of those who attended the performances began to assemble, or copy, the works they had heard performed. A notable collector of the songs during Schubert's lifetime was Karl Pinterics, a man somewhat at odds with the bohemian assortment of Schubert's close friends. A man of cultivated taste who worked as a private secretary to the nobility, he was also a fine pianist and ardent admirer of Schubert who himself hosted Schubertiads at his lodgings. He collected and catalogued a total of 505 *lieder* by the time of his own death in 1831, the first of a number of collectors who were each to add their contribution to the task of collecting and recording the *lieder*. Sadly, he had no opportunity to hear or appreciate the rich collection of orchestral and other works which remained unrecorded and unheard at the time of his death.

Pinterics' collection was then acquired by Josef Witteczek, a lawyer who subsequently built a successful career in government service. Witteczek had shared lodgings with Josef von Spaun in the house of Professor Heinrich Watteroth where Schubert, in 1816, recorded proudly that he had received his first paid commission – for the cantata *Prometheus*, which was performed by Watteroth's pupils in his honour. While the performance was a success, the manuscript was later lost and remains to this day unknown – sadly a fate which befell other works although the great majority of Schubert's compositions were eventually recovered. Schubert was a few years junior to Witteczek and von Spaun but they and the professor became ardent enthusiasts for Schubert's music and participated in Schubertiads in each of their residences over the coming years. Witteczek himself added to the collection of *lieder* including copies of many other shorter works. He died in 1859 having bequeathed what was by then the principal collection of original *lieder* to his and Schubert's mutual and loyal friend, Josef von Spaun.

Von Spaun, after a successful career in government service, and having been created a baron, died in 1865 leaving the *lieder* collection to the Vienna Gesellschaft der Musikfreunde where it remains today. Von Spaun was without doubt the most loyal, the most reliable as well as the most well-informed of Schubert's personal acquaintances and left several detailed accounts of the composer and his life, much of which is referred to in these pages. One of his notable contributions is his critical comments on the biography by von Hellborn where, in addition to correcting factual errors, his verdict was that the book 'contains too little light and too much shade about Schubert the man.' Von Hellborn's biography features in a later chapter.

Ferdinand died in Vienna in 1859 still with the iron chest containing a sizeable number of manuscripts. Some of these were acquired by the Gesellschaft der Musikfreunde but the bulk passed to Schubert's nephew Eduard Schneider, son of his sister Maria Theresia. It was these manuscripts that would be inspected in 1867, as we shall see, by George Grove, when he and Arthur Sullivan visited Vienna in search of missing works. The pair discovered the original orchestral parts of the *Singspiel Rosamunde*. They also found the scores of all but one of the symphonies, which had laid undisturbed for almost half a century, attracting no interest despite Ferdinand's valiant efforts. The exception was Symphony No 5, of which Ferdinand had earlier made a copy which he presented to the Gesellschaft der Musikfreunde, where it was inspected by Grove. Ferdinand had also made a copy of Symphony No 6, the work that had been performed in place of the *Great* C Major Symphony in 1828 and again in 1829.

CLOSE OF A DECADE

The first decade after the death of Franz Schubert thus ends with Ferdinand, in 1839, writing the first of what was to become many personal accounts of the composer's life, in this case with the added interest of an enlarged list of the compositions which Ferdinand himself had also compiled. The works were marked as 'Sch' if still in his possession and 'D' if in the hands of Messrs Diabelli. The compositions were arranged in years thus forming the first, albeit far from accurate or comprehensive, catalogue of Schubert's output. The list confirms what appears from other sources, that in Ferdinand's chest there still lay the bulk of the symphonies, the operas and the masses, while most of the unpublished *lieder*, the quartets and piano works had been sent to Diabelli. The manuscripts acquired by the publisher included the great String Quintet and the three piano sonatas of the final year; in the case of the sonatas, works that were to remain in the shadows for many years. One wonders what Schubert himself would have thought of the way in which his life's work was arbitrarily divided and sold off piecemeal. Perhaps he would have been reminded of the division of Christ's garment.

The collection or accumulation of Schubert's manuscripts is described above. But in addition to preservation there was an increasing need to catalogue the works, particularly the *lieder*. Ferdinand had made a start in 1835 when listing the compositions available for performance. His work was taken up after 1845 by Aloys Fuchs, a civil servant and musicologist who had amassed a huge collection of artefacts and manuscripts of many earlier composers, but who now decided to add Schubert to his range of interests by making a collection of notes for the beginnings of a thematic catalogue. From 1850 Josef Witteczek, who as we have seen then held the most extensive collection of *lieder* manuscripts, added further notes to Fuchs' original catalogue, and took the opportunity of incorporating Karl Pinterics' original catalogue of 1830, listing the 505 *lieder* he had collected. As will be seen, the accurate collating of the works, to say nothing of their performance, was to stretch some decades into the future.

PART II REAWAKENING

CHAPTER 5
THREE COMPOSERS

So far in this story, the burden of preserving and bringing to the public's attention the masterpieces left behind by the dead composer had fallen almost exclusively on Ferdinand Schubert in the 10 years after his brother's death. The Viennese public, perhaps no more fickle and fashion-driven than any other urban population of the nineteenth century, or of any other age, had responded enthusiastically to the beauties of the *lieder* and a few other incidental works but had then moved on to the thrills of Rossini and Paganini. The dead Schubert remained in danger of being passed over and forgotten.

Ferdinand's sterling efforts to secure either publication or performance of many of the greatest creations left by the composer had met with little success. But there were other forces at work which would, within a few years, bring about great change, in the shape of three major musical figures of the age. Of these three, who are about to make their entrance, two were German but the first was Hungarian.

FRANZ LISZT

Some 14 years younger than Schubert, their paths crossed in Vienna in 1822–3 where the famously precocious Hungarian piano virtuoso and composer studied, inter alia, with Salieri. Liszt and Schubert almost certainly would have met, but there is no record of such an event. Liszt is said to have been introduced to Schubert's *lieder* by Baron Schönstein, who was the most important interpreter of the songs after Vogl. What is clear is that the young Liszt became familiar with Schubert's *lieder* and dances, probably during Schubert's lifetime, and from 1833 produced a series of transcriptions or pastiches of many of the greatest *lieder*, eventually totalling more than 60 and including many from the three great song cycles. There can be no doubt that Liszt's celebrity and concert performances of his transcriptions were a material force in the spread of Schubert's music throughout Europe from the 1830s. This would, of course, have served to reinforce Schubert's fame as a composer of *lieder*, but of little else. In the coming years and decades, publishers collected and engraved more and more *lieder* to be sold, not just in Vienna but to a wider European audience. It was no wonder, therefore, that Schubert's reputation remained established as a song composer. Liszt's paraphrase of *Erlkönig*, performed in Vienna in 1838 and also in Leipzig, is said to have been rapturously received, no doubt as an improvement on the original.

Franz Liszt, born into the family of a minor Hungarian court official, showed such prodigious talent from an early age that he gained sponsors to further his musical education, eventually leading to the move to Vienna in 1821. Here he gave concerts attended, inter alia, by Beethoven and embarked on his own compositions from the age of 12, such that he was invited (along with Schubert) to contribute a variation to the famous set commissioned by the publisher Diabelli. In 1823 the Liszt family moved to Paris, from where the young Franz continued to give concerts and then toured throughout Europe including London.

His celebrity was such that he met the leading composers of the time, including Berlioz and Chopin, and mixed in the best social circles. His far from discreet affair with Countess Marie d'Agoult produced three children including a daughter Cosima, who was later to marry Richard Wagner, who thus became Liszt's son-in-law. Liszt was everything that Schubert was not – a phenomenal performer and accomplished socialite. But Liszt's enduring celebrity served Schubert's memory well after his early death, by continuing to spread his music, limited to the *lieder* and in Liszt's own transcriptions, throughout Europe.

In later years Liszt devoted himself to the promotion of works other than *lieder* and dances, which included organising a performance of *Alfonso und Estrella* in 1854 as well as orchestral arrangements, to which we will return. Liszt was truly devoted to Schubert's compositions, perhaps perceiving depths absent from his own music. Liszt spoke of Schubert as 'the most poetic musician who ever lived,' a view that was certainly not universal at the time, although it is readily acceptable today. The great service that Liszt performed for posterity was to ensure from the 1830s onwards that Schubert's music and reputation would be carried all round Europe at a pace far beyond what could be achieved by the publishing and selling of sheet music. Whether or not through the influence of Liszt, who lived in Paris up to 1835, translations of the *lieder* began to appear in French from 1833; and by 1850 C. S. Richault in Paris is said to have published 367 songs in French translation, in 16 volumes. The spread of *lieder* in France even led to Hector Berlioz composing an orchestration of *Erlkönig*, the song that Liszt continued to perform throughout Europe.

Up to the end of 1838 little attention had been paid to the *Great* C Major Symphony, now recognised as one of Schubert's iconic achievements but shrouded in mystery up to the 1980s and beyond as to its true date of composition. The work had been largely ignored through the first decade after the composer's death and certainly never performed. Now, with the intervention of two more celebrated supporters, all that was to change.

ROBERT SCHUMANN

Described by O. E. Deutsch as 'one of the first and most enthusiastic champions of Schubert's art,' Robert Schumann was born in 1810 but never met Schubert. By 1828, Schumann was an accomplished pianist who knew and admired Schubert's *Wanderer* Fantasia (D760) and many of the published dances and other piano works. He recorded having written a letter to Schubert, which was never sent and was lost. When Schumann heard of Schubert's death, only in November 1830, his then companion, Emil Flechsig, reported that sobbing was heard all through the night.

Schumann had heard and admired one of the piano trios at the house of Friedrich Wieck, who in due course was to become his reluctant father-in-law. In 1835, in response to Ferdinand's invitation to subscribe for performing rights in the collection of unpublished works still in his possession, Schumann had not responded directly but had reprinted Ferdinand's advertisement in the *Neue Zeitschrift für Musik* in a vain attempt to drum up enthusiasm for the unpublished works, none of which he had then seen. Subsequently, in late 1838 he decided to fulfil an ambition to visit Vienna with the intention of considering a relocation. It was by chance that he found himself, on 1 January 1839, paying a visit to Ferdinand and inspecting the manuscripts in the famous chest. Schumann recalled the list of works in the possession of Ferdinand comprising operas, masses and seven symphonies, being those now numbered 1 to 6 plus the *Great* C Major.

Schumann's first 29 years, up until 1829, had packed in all the drama and travel that Schubert's short life had not. He was at that stage enmeshed in his passionate affair with Clara Wieck, whose father was vehemently opposed to their marriage and was later to be joined in court proceedings over the match. Clara, now a celebrated pianist in her own right, already enjoyed a high reputation in Vienna and the couple had contemplated moving to the Austrian capital. However there were many details to be settled, including finding a new publisher for the *Neue Zeitschrift*, of which Robert remained editor. In the end, none of these schemes came to fruition and he was obliged to return to Leipzig in April 1839 because of family affairs. The visit to Ferdinand, therefore, proved to be the notable success of the trip, during which Robert continued his compositions at a rate that even matched that of Schubert himself, and included, as might be expected, movements of his *Faschingsschwank aus Wien*.

Upon making the acquaintance of Ferdinand and examining the manuscripts in the chest, Schumann was reportedly amazed by the high quality of the works he inspected, particularly by the *Great* C Major Symphony, of which he examined the copy Ferdinand himself had made some time in 1827 or 1828. So it was that, at Schumann's suggestion, scores of both the *Great* C Major and Symphony No 6, of which Ferdinand had also made a copy, were sent to the publishers Breitkopf & Härtel in Leipzig. The publisher sent the manuscripts on to Mendelssohn, then conductor of the Leipzig Gewandhaus Orchestra, who was to give the *Great* C Major Symphony its first performance, in 1839. The orchestral parts were then published in 1840, the first of any of the symphonies in print. Mendelssohn was to perform the work no less than 12 times during his life.

Schumann wrote an account of his visit to Ferdinand in an article for the *Neue Zeitschrift für Musik*, which was subsequently published in a collection entitled *Music and Musicians* in 1853. The article is lavish in its praise of the *Great* C Major Symphony, noting particularly the great skill of the orchestration and expressing his admiration for the work in the following comments:

It reveals to us something more than mere fine melody, mere ordinary joy and sorrow, such as music has already expressed in a hundred ways – that it leads us into a region which we never before explored, and consequently can have no recollection of. Here we find, besides the most masterly technicalities of musical composition, life in every vein, colouring down to the finest grade of possibility, sharp expression in detail, meaning throughout, while over the whole is thrown that glow of romanticism that everywhere accompanies Franz Schubert. And then the heavenly length of the symphony … .

The symphony produced such an effect among us, as none has produced since Beethoven's. Artists and connoisseurs united in its praise, and I heard a few words spoken by the master who had studied it [Mendelssohn] with the utmost care for its perfect success, that I should have been only too happy, had such a thing been possible, to report to the living Schubert, as the gladdest of glad tidings. Years must pass, perhaps, before the work will be thoroughly made at home in Germany; but there is no danger that it will ever be overlooked or forgotten; it bears within it the core of everlasting youth.*

In the same commentary Schumann lavishes praise on the D Minor Quartet and the E flat Piano Trio, although his view of the recently published Grand Duo in C, Opus 140, is somewhat mixed. His review then turns to the Opus 142 Impromptus, which had been published in 1839. Schumann's firm conviction was that the first two Impromptus, in F Minor and A flat, formed the first and second movements of a sonata, of which the fourth, also in F Minor, would make a lively close. Sadly he concluded that the third, the variations on a theme from *Rosamunde*, was inferior and 'wholly devoid of invention.' (He appears to have overlooked Beethoven's choice of variations in the *Eroica* Symphony and elsewhere, and indeed Schubert's own liking for

---

* R Schumann, *Neue Zeitschrift für Musik*, 1843.

the medium). The commentary on the last three piano sonatas is even more surprising. It is convenient to address the works here since little or nothing would be heard of these masterpieces until the advent of the twentieth century, astonishing as that might seem given their current standing. Having been published in 1838 at the same time as the Opus 142 Impromptus, Schumann's assessment of the sonatas was the following:

> I cannot learn whether he wrote these sonatas on his sick-bed or not; from the music I rather surmise that he did; and yet it may be that one's opinion and fancy are influenced beforehand by the sad ideas awakened by the word 'last' on the title-page. However it may be, these sonatas seem to me to differ from his others in their greater simplicity of invention, their voluntary resignation of novel brilliancy (just where he formerly made such great demands on his powers), and through a general spinning out of musical ideas where he formerly joined period to period with new threads. It flows on from page to page, ever more musical and melodious, as if it could never come to an end or lose its continuity, broken, here and there, by a somewhat more lively emotion, that is, however, soon quieted again. Colder judges must decide whether or not my opinion has been influenced here by the thought of his illness; but the work affects me as I describe it.

It is tempting to speculate how far this well-circulated view of the works led to their being largely ignored for the next 60 years. Schumann remains, however, forever redeemed by the part he played, just over a decade after the composer's death, in bringing the *Great* C Major Symphony to life and sending it on its way to the immortality that has been its proper place since 1839.

FELIX MENDELSSOHN

Unlike Schumann, there is no indication that Mendelssohn had any earlier connection or even knowledge of Schubert's works. Born in 1809 and raised in a well-to-do family of Jewish bankers and philosophers in Berlin, he was a true child prodigy. His performing abilities were celebrated but above all his precocious composing skills produced works such as the famous Octet for Strings of 1825, when aged 16. After extensive travels which included England, Scotland and Italy, Mendelssohn settled in Leipzig as a conductor of the celebrated Gewandhaus Orchestra with which he directed the first and many subsequent performances of the *Great* C Major Symphony.

Mendelssohn was a near contemporary of Robert Schumann. The two became acquainted both professionally and socially, and both admired the prodigious talent of Clara Wieck, who was finally to marry Robert Schumann in 1840. Clara had already appeared regularly as soloist at the Gewandhaus and in concert halls throughout Europe. Mendelssohn had taken up his appointment in Leipzig in 1835 after appearances with many other orchestras. His major contribution to the musical life of Leipzig was, first, the reorganisation and upgrading of the Gewandhaus Orchestra, in which he was the first to adopt the modern role of conductor rather than leaving direction to the orchestra's leader. Secondly, he had embarked, even before the Leipzig appointment, on the revival of great music of past eras including particularly the works of J. S. Bach, much of which had been composed for, and performed in, Leipzig churches. The range of music performed under Mendelssohn included Mozart and Beethoven, as well as contemporary composers. So it was peculiarly fortunate that it was Robert Schumann who unearthed the *Great* C Major Symphony, and particularly fortunate that he was able to direct the work to Mendelssohn whose orchestra, unlike those of Vienna and subsequently other cities, was able to take on the unique challenges posed by the symphony, particularly to the string players.

Mendelssohn, the first conductor to perform the *Great* C Major Symphony

As we have seen, Ferdinand had dispatched, at Schumann's request, copies of the manuscripts of the *Great* C Major Symphony (D944) and of Symphony No 6 (D589) to Leipzig where the publisher passed the scores on to Mendelssohn for his assessment. On studying the manuscripts Mendelssohn, like Schumann, was overcome with admiration for the qualities of the hitherto unknown works and determined to organise a performance of the *Great* C Major, which took place swiftly on 21 March 1839, while Schumann was still in Vienna. Mendelssohn was less impressed by the 'heavenly length' and considered that some of the marked repeats should not necessarily be followed.

Otherwise it appears the symphony was performed in its entirety (and not in a heavily truncated form as reported elsewhere) and was enthusiastically received by both players and audience. Mendelssohn recorded its reception in a letter to Ferdinand:

> There was great and sustained applause after each movement and, more important than that, all the musicians in the orchestra were moved and delighted by the splendid work. It has had more success than most of the new works during the last four years and we are going to repeat it at the very beginning of the next series of concerts.

Further performances were given in Leipzig on 12 December 1839, this time attended by Schumann, and again on 26 October 1840. Mendelssohn continued to correspond with Ferdinand who, in gratitude for his championing of the *Great* C Major, made him a gift of the Symphony in E Major (D729), sketched in orchestral score, which had been composed in 1821 and then laid aside never to be revisited, at least not by Schubert. Mendelssohn wrote a letter of thanks to Ferdinand in which he said of Franz Schubert:

> It seems to me as if, through the very incompleteness of the work, through the scattered half finished indications, I got to know your brother personally, and more closely and more intimately than I could have done through a finished piece. It is as if I saw him there working in his room.

Thus the story progresses into the 1840s and, while in 1830 Ferdinand was almost alone in his quest to bring his brother's music before the public, by the end of the decade he had been joined by these three powerful and enthusiastic champions. Liszt was to play his transcriptions throughout Europe and to orchestrate works of Schubert which, in his hands, were guaranteed an audience. His admiration for Schubert's music also led to the first performance in 1854 of *Alfonso und Estrella* in Weimar. Schumann had achieved the breakthrough in bringing the *Great* C Major Symphony, perhaps the most iconic of Schubert's grandest works, to Leipzig for its performance and publication. And Mendelssohn, not content with then having performed the symphony twice in Leipzig, took it to Paris and to London in 1845. In both venues he encountered resistance from orchestral players to the difficulties of performing what Schubert had written.

But at least the message was clear, that Schubert, contrary to what the Viennese had known of him, was a major orchestral composer. It is of interest that the work was performed, apparently without resistance from orchestral players, in Boston and in New York in 1849. Where Schubert had previously been accepted as a composer of *lieder* and piano works, he was now seen as a symphonist and composer of major orchestral works. However, while the *Great* C Major Symphony had been performed and was on the way to being accepted as a major part of the international musical repertoire, there still remained the treasure trove of manuscripts in Ferdinand's chest in Vienna. They still awaited the rescuers who would continue the process of unearthing the true achievements of Franz Schubert.

CHAPTER 6
THE VIENNESE SCHUBERTIANS

While three celebrated composers had achieved the breakthrough that had eluded the enlightened music lovers of Vienna, Schubert's own city awaited similar champions to address the task of revealing the music of its native composer. The wait would soon lead to action, but not without resistance. Fortunately for posterity, the Viennese champions, while not of the same celebrity as Liszt, Schumann or Mendelssohn, were all influential musicians.

Schubert's Viennese supporters were individuals who became what today would be called Schubertians – persons who came to admire and love Schubert's music to the extent that they felt impelled to share the pleasure with others and to promote the music to those not yet able to enjoy its beauties. As will be seen, prominent Schubertians were to appear in different countries and at different times but their appearance in Vienna in the two decades after the death was to prove a major step forward in the dissemination of the music.

FURTHER ATTEMPTS AT PERFORMANCE

No doubt inspired by Schumann's musical journalism, as well as by news of the Leipzig performances, the Viennese musical authorities were prodded into a further attempt to perform the *Great* C Major Symphony, as the first endeavour at the memorial concert in December 1828 had failed. The finale of the symphony was successfully performed in Vienna in 1836 but no full performance was projected until 15 December 1839, 11 years after the performance planned during Schubert's lifetime. But this again was abandoned for lack of rehearsal time, despite the work having been performed in Leipzig earlier the same year. The symphony was taken up again by the French conductor François Habeneck in 1842, when only the first movement was reportedly given. The performance was recalled in a memoir of Eduard Schneider, Schubert's nephew and future inheritor of the collection of manuscripts, who wrote in 1857 as follows:

> Habeneck's attempt to perform the symphony, at which I was present, came to an end with the first movement. The orchestra of the Conservatoire resisted all attempts to persuade it even to play the second movement.

Perhaps Habeneck was not yet a true Schubertian. At all events, Vienna was not alone. When the same conductor in 1843 attempted to perform the symphony in Paris, the violinists reportedly rebelled at being asked to play 88 bars of triplets in the final movement. Even Mendelssohn had had the same experience in London in 1843 when attempting to rehearse the symphony for a philharmonic concert. However, a change of fortune was approaching for Vienna.

FAMILY HELLMESBERGER

Georg Hellmesberger was a near-contemporary of Schubert who had been a fellow pupil at the Stadtkonvikt in 1810–12. He followed a distinguished musical career as professor at the Vienna Conservatory, concert master at the court opera and conductor at the Gesellschaft der Musikfreunde. His son, Josef, born in 1828, a few days before Schubert's death, was to follow an even more celebrated musical career as both performer and conductor in a series of concerts that would achieve lasting fame in Vienna and elsewhere for the exceptional quality of their performances. Although not a matter of record, Josef and his father were doubtless aware, through Ferdinand's published catalogue, of the chamber music still awaiting publication and in the possession of the publisher Diabelli. Josef was able to obtain the manuscripts and, certainly with the encouragement of the publisher, to arrange performances of the works.

Thus the Hellmesberger Quartet, on 11 November 1849 and led by the 21-year-old Josef, gave the first performance in Vienna since the composer's death of the Quartet in D Minor, *Death and the Maiden* (D810). In the following year, on 17 November 1850, the augmented quartet gave the first ever performance of the great String Quintet (D956). A mere two weeks later, on 1 December 1850, Georg Hellmesberger conducted the orchestra of the Musikfreunde in the first complete performance in Vienna of the *Great* C Major Symphony.

We have seen that the finale of the symphony had been performed in Vienna in 1836 and the first movement in 1842, but with this first full performance, the Viennese had finally caught up with Leipzig, after a decade. And a week later, on 8 December 1850, the Hellmesberger Quartet gave the first complete performance of the G Major Quartet (D887). The first movement had been given at Schubert's benefit concert in March 1828 but nothing further had been heard of the work, which had languished on the publisher's shelves along with the String

Quintet and other works since Schubert's death. Through these performances the Hellmesberger family generated a renewed interest in Schubert's hitherto unheard chamber and orchestral works that would, in the following years, add to the growing realisation of the true greatness of Vienna's home-grown composer.

This sudden flowering in Vienna of interest in Schubert's previously unheard compositions led rapidly to publication of the G Major Quartet and the String Quintet, as well as the Octet (D803), all of which had been published by 1853. The growing fame of the Hellmesberger Quartet, which also played the late works of Beethoven, led to many more performances of Schubert's chamber works and to the publication of his earlier unpublished and unperformed quartets. While the ensemble performed widely throughout Europe, Josef Hellmesberger remained a devotee and enthusiastic promoter of Schubert's music throughout his long life. His exceptional memory is said to have allowed him, as a pianist, to accompany all of the *lieder* without the aid of a score. It was at his suggestion that the remains of both Schubert and Beethoven were exhumed and reinterred in new metal coffins in October 1863. Josef also became one of the editors of the *Gesamtausgabe* from 1884 until his death in 1893.

As a postscript to the Vienna performance of December 1850, the first full performance of the *Great* C Major Symphony in Paris took place in 1851. The work was first heard in London in 1856 under Augustus Manns at the Crystal Palace, having by then already been performed in New York and Boston.

JOHAN VON HERBECK

Johann von Herbeck was another notable Viennese musician, appointed in 1856 as choirmaster of the prominent mens part song society, the Männergesang-Verein. The society, which continues today, had been formed in 1845 and regularly performed many of Schubert's compositions for male voices. A major festival of choral societies was held in Vienna on 19 November 1847, the anniversary of Schubert's death. Herbeck was subsequently appointed director of the Singverein, the mixed choir of the Gesellschaft der Musikfreunde; orchestral conductor at the Musikfreunde, and director of the Vienna Court Opera.

Throughout his career Herbeck venerated Schubert, championing in particular the male voice part songs. As well as performing the known repertoire, he was responsible for rescuing many works from oblivion, including a performance in 1862 of *Lazarus* (D689), which had not been heard since 1830. Herbeck was a tireless promoter of Schubert's music in choral societies throughout Austria and Germany and organised orchestral performances including the *Great* C Major Symphony and Liszt's orchestral arrangement of the *Wanderer* Fantasia.

It was Herbeck's proposal to the Männergesang-Verein that led to the commissioning of the statue of Schubert in the Vienna Stadtpark for which the laying of the foundation stone took place in October 1868, and the unveiling in May 1872. Finance for the statue was raised by the Männergesang-Verein via fundraising concerts in which Josef Hellmesberger performed, as well as from private donations, principally from the philanthropist Nikolaus Dumba. However Herbeck's greatest contribution and greatest satisfaction came in 1865 with his personal intervention to persuade Anselm Hüttenbrenner to part with the manuscript of the *Unfinished* Symphony in B Minor (D759). The symphony had come to light either as a result of a letter from brother Josef Hüttenbrenner or as a consequence of the von Hellborn biography, published in 1863, which revealed its hitherto unknown existence. It was Herbeck who obtained the manuscript and he that conducted the first performance of this incomparable work. The performance took place at the Musikverein on 17 December 1865, creating a tide of new interest and enthusiasm for Schubert's works and the *Unfinished* in particular. His exploits led to international recognition, such that even Hector Berlioz in Paris commended his talents as a conductor.

So, in the third decade after Schubert's death, it seems the musical forces of Vienna were finally moving towards recognising and beginning to repay the great debt they owed to the genius they had overlooked during his lifetime, and to rethink the reputation they had collectively bestowed on Franz Schubert as a composer only of *lieder*. It should not be supposed that this was in any way a smooth transition: life in Vienna remained as uncertain as it had been during Napoleonic times.

REVOLUTION IN EUROPE

Throughout the 1840s the city of Vienna had been busily burnishing its reputation, no longer as the city of Mozart and Beethoven, but as the international home of 'Viennese' waltzes and the cheap popular culture led by the Strauss family. Compared to this new industrial-scale culture, the patient rediscovery of the works of Franz Schubert remained a fringe activity. But outside the world of music, all was not well within the Austro-Hungarian Empire, nor within much of Europe which still laboured under the repercussions of the European settlement agreed and imposed at the Congress of Vienna in 1815. There had been unrest in Paris in 1830 and now in February 1848 a full-scale uprising broke out, fuelled by widespread social problems. Similar uprisings broke out in many other European capitals; those in Italy being of particular concern to Austria as the occupying power. Unrest in Vienna rapidly followed in March 1848, mostly fuelled by unemployment and poverty. Within days, the longstanding government minister and effective dictator, Prince Metternich, fled from the city with his family, en route to London. Attempts to quell the unrest failed and in May 1848 insurgents based at the university effectively took control of the city.

By this time the Emperor and his court had left the city and taken refuge in Innsbruck. Imperial troops were fully engaged in seeking to control risings in other parts of the empire, including Prague; and the situation in Hungary was confused and violent. But by August the situation in Vienna had stabilised so that the Imperial family were able to return. However, insurgents remained in occupation of the centre of the city and were determined to resist a return to government control. In October, the Emperor and his court were once more forced to withdraw as Imperial forces laid siege to the old city of Vienna. All attempts to reach a compromise failed and Vienna then suffered a full-scale military assault with much destruction and loss of life. Fortunately, resistance was short-lived and life in the city was soon able to return to relative normality. So it was that the performances of hitherto unheard works of Franz Schubert given by members of the Hellmesberger family from late 1849 were the best possible indication that life in Vienna was continuing, and that the rehabilitation of Schubert's music could continue.

One notable and, as it turned out, long-lasting memory from the unrest of 1848 was the commemoration of the exploits of Field Marshal Radetzky, who successfully commanded the Imperial Austrian forces in Italy. Johann Strauss was not slow to compose his *Radetzky March*, which has continued in its popularity to this day, whenever played in public. It is tempting to compare the enthusiastic hand-clapping of the Viennese with the full-throated singing of *Land of Hope and Glory* at the Last Night of the Proms in London; although it must be said that the Austrian Empire in Italy was to last no more than another two decades. And it might also be added that Johann Strauss was no Elgar.

CHAPTER 7
INTO THE 1850S

The previous chapter unavoidably jumped ahead to the 1860s but we now return to earlier events. The 1850s saw a gradual but steady growth of interest in the emerging musical treasures left by the composer. By 1850 Mendelssohn was dead and from 1854 Schumann was confined to a mental asylum. However, Franz Liszt was now at the height of his powers and continued to perform his arrangements of Schubert's works, not limited to *lieder*, and to promote the music of the dead composer. His arrangements included the orchestral version of the *Wanderer* Fantasia, rewritten as the piano concerto that Schubert never found the opportunity to write. His interest in Schubert's works included the operas and led to his organising a first performance of *Alfonso und Estrella* in Weimar, after much rearrangement of the score, on 24 June 1854.

We should be reminded at this point that Schubert's conviction that the path to public recognition was through grand opera was not misplaced. Carl Maria von Weber, only 10 years senior to Schubert, had been responsible for introducing grand romantic opera in German, temporarily superseding Italian opera, in Berlin and Dresden, with *Der Freischütz*. He then moved to Vienna for a production of *Euryanthe* in 1823, where he memorably encountered Schubert, whose well-recorded remarks resulted in somewhat frosty relations between the two composers thereafter.* In 1826, while on a visit to London for a production of *Oberon* at Covent Garden, Weber died and with him, the immediate prospect of German opera taking off again in Vienna. As we have seen, Schubert, in the 1820s, struggled with his own operas against the tide of Italian opera led in Vienna by Rossini, while his fellow countryman Vincenzo Bellini, a near contemporary of Schubert, achieved great success with his operas in Italy and finally in Paris, before his untimely death in 1835.

By this date Richard Wagner's plans for his first successful German operas, *Rienzi* and *Der fliegende Holländer*, were well advanced. They would shortly be performed in Munich, followed by *Tannhäuser* and *Lohengrin* which served to establish grand opera sung in German as one of the great musical phenomena of the mid and late-nineteenth century. And from 1839 Giuseppe Verdi was producing grand operas in Italian which would fill opera houses throughout Europe in the 1850s and 60s.

Nor were circumstances in the mid-nineteenth century propitious for the success of Schubert's works in other forms of music. Opera was to remain in the headlines throughout most of the nineteenth century, but other musical genres continued their development. Liszt continued his concert performances as the most famous pianist of the century, and the piano repertoire in the 1840s was also dominated by Chopin. His performances had failed to captivate the Viennese but he became widely successful in Paris where, unlike Schubert, he gained recognition as a celebrated composer. The 1850s saw the gradual emergence of the music of Johannes Brahms, whose abilities had earlier been recognised by the Schumanns, and Brahms was to dominate the symphonic world as the successor to Beethoven during the

---

* See further Chapter 18.

remainder of the century. The second half of the nineteenth century represented perhaps the most significant flowering of musical compositions throughout Europe. It was against this background that the continuing endeavours of a few enthusiasts to rescue the works of Franz Schubert from obscurity need to be viewed, particularly piano music following the success of Schumann, Liszt and Chopin.

ALFONSO UND ESTRELLA

As we have seen, Ferdinand had recovered the original manuscript of the opera from the Pachler family in Graz in 1842 and, at the request of Franz von Schober, Schubert's erstwhile friend and the opera's librettist, the score of *Alfonso und Estrella* was sent on to Liszt, for whom the same Schober was now working as an assistant. Liszt, however, while admiring the music, formed a low opinion of the libretto and reportedly considered having the story rewritten to fit the music; an interesting idea that was not pursued at that time. The story of the opera can be read in some detail in von Hellborn's biography.* It concerns a dispossessed monarch, heroic warriors and a beautiful heroine. Alfonso is the exiled son of the former monarch who meets and becomes enamoured with Estrella, who is the daughter of the general of the usurper, Adolfo, who is also determined to win the beautiful Estrella. In the course of the ensuing battles, Adolfo carries Estrella away, but Alfonso appears with a band of loyal warriors, captures Adolfo and in the outcome the king is restored to his kingdom. The king hands the kingdom over to Alfonso and the general similarly hands over his daughter to a universal chorus of rejoicing peasants and soldiers.

Von Hellborn also presents a synopsis of the musical numbers, as with other operas, and gives his opinion on the merits of the music in which he finds much to praise. Some

---

* English translation, Vol I, p 235-245.

scenes 'showed an extraordinary skill in his mastery over the grand forms of the musical drama.' However, the opera as a whole suffered from one patent defect, namely that the grand dramatic element was entirely wanting in the libretto, for which the blame is naturally laid at Schubert's door. For other reasons the opera was never staged in Vienna or elsewhere in Schubert's lifetime, but was given its first ever performance in 1854 in truncated form, which did not result in it being taken up by other opera houses, and the work remained sidelined for the remainder of the nineteenth century and well beyond.

Liszt's interest in Schubert's emerging works also led him to consider writing what would be the first biography, and to this end Liszt, in 1854, solicited a memoir from Anselm Hüttenbrenner, as well as one from Ferdinand. He also began to organise a collection of Schubert's works with a view to creating a catalogue. Neither project came to fruition, no doubt as a result of the complexity of the task he had embarked on and Liszt's busy musical life as a performer and composer. However, he retained his interest in Schubert's music, which he continued to promote throughout Europe, largely through the medium of his own arrangements of *lieder* and dances.

MORE PERFORMANCES

We have seen that the major chamber works, including the String Quintet, were given public performances in 1850 by the Hellmesberger Quartet. The quintet is reported to have been performed 14 times by the same players and is said to have circulated widely through Europe after its publication in 1853, receiving its Paris premiere in February 1866. Another distinguished quartet, led by Joseph Joachim, the celebrated soloist in the first performance of the Brahms Violin Concerto, was formed in 1869 and is said to have performed the String Quintet 16 times from 1870.

The *Great* C Major Symphony, after its performances in

Leipzig and finally in Vienna in 1850, was taken up in Paris and London during the 1850s, and had reached the United States, where performances took place in Boston and New York. Schubert's reputation in these and many other major cultural centres was already well established as a composer of *lieder*; but he was now beginning to be recognised as a major composer in other genres, whether of chamber music, piano compositions or orchestral works. Yet even with this wider recognition there was, as yet, no conception of the full range of compositions, nor of the huge store of works, including symphonies, masses and operas, still awaiting discovery and performance.

It is understandable that the task of bringing together the plethora of compositions should take many years. The works had to be copied and performed and then published, in each case requiring the performers or publishers to be confident of securing an audience and public interest. Even in Vienna, where the majority of performances of new works took place, the pace of bringing out new works was necessarily gradual. There is no doubt, though, that the public had an appetite for more works of Schubert. The extensive records that exist of the appearance of new works in Vienna from the 1850s and early 1860s show first performances including: the complete *Die schöne Müllerin* (D795) in May 1856; arias from *Fierrabras* (D796) in February 1858; the Grand Duo for piano duet in C Major (D812) in December 1859; the final movement (only) of Symphony No 3 (D200) in December 1860; the overture to *Des Teufels Lustschloss* (D84) in March 1861; the Adagio and Rondo Concertante for Piano Quartet (D487) in November 1861; the String Quartet in B flat (D112) in February 1862; choruses from *Fierrabras* (D796) in December 1862; the early String Quartet in G Minor (D173) in November 1863; and excerpts from *Der Graf von Gleichen* (D918) in December 1865.*

Johann von Herbeck, as we have seen, was the most active of

---

* See Janet I Wasserman, 'First Performances,' *The Schubertian* April 2009 p 9-21.

promoters of Schubert's music in Vienna and elsewhere. He presented regular concerts including Schubert's music, both vocal and orchestral, between 1857 and the 1870s. As conductor of the Männergesang-Verein he presented male voice part songs, some of which he had discovered or rescued. In October 1858 he conducted a performance of the Quartet *Die Einsiedelei* (D337) in front of Schubert's birthplace in Währing, which had recently been designated as a monument.

The part songs performed by the Männergesang-Verein included *Gesang der Geister über den Wassern* (D704), *Die Nacht* (D983), *Sehnsucht* (D656) and *Wein und Liebe* (D901). In March 1863, Herbeck conducted a performance of *Lazarus* (D689), which had not been heard since 1830. Then, as conductor of the Gesellschaft der Musikfreunde, he performed the *Great* C Major Symphony and the *Wanderer* Fantasia in Liszt's orchestral version. He even organised a performance in 1874 with Liszt as soloist. Herbeck conducted the first concert version in March 1861 of the *Singspiel Die Verschworenen* (D787), a first staged performance being given subsequently in Frankfurt am Main in August 1861. As conductor of the court Kapelle, Herbeck performed Schubert's masses, No 2 in G (D167) in December 1865, the final E flat Mass (D950) in August 1866, and the Mass in A flat (D678) in April 1869.*

A STATUE IS PROPOSED

It was Herbeck's championing of Schubert's music that led the Männergesang-Verein to give its support to a project to erect a statue of the composer in the Stadtpark. For this project he conducted a special concert in support of the memorial in March 1865 in which the *Great* C Major Symphony was performed together with extracts from *Rosamunde* and a number of *lieder*. This proved effective in gathering the further financial support

---

* *Ibid.*

needed, which in particular included support from the politician, philanthropist and patron of the arts, Nikolaus Dumba, who was also vice-president of the Gesellschaft der Musikfreunde and president of the Männergesang-Verein. Herbeck conducted an open-air concert to mark the laying of the foundation stone for the monument in October 1868.

It seems a little odd today that the only life-size monument to Schubert should be in celebration of his fame as a composer of male-voice part songs. It nonetheless tells us something of the level of enthusiasm which Schubert's music gave rise to, an enthusiasm not limited to listening but embracing the joy of participating in performances, as witnessed by the continuing popularity of the Männergesang-Verein.

Thirty years after his death, despite the slow rise in popularity of his music, Franz Schubert's brief life remained in obscurity. But plans were afoot for even more ambitious projects, which would finally establish the composer's reputation beyond question.

CHAPTER 8
THE 1860S: A BIOGRAPHY AND A SYMPHONY

In the months and years following Schubert's death many friends and acquaintances, realising the need to remember and record the dead composer, began to write and exchange biographical notes. As time went by several individuals independently conceived the idea of collecting and soliciting such memorials with a view to working up a biography, including Franz Liszt as we have seen. The memorials paint an engaging picture of the man and his music and were collected and published, principally in a volume assembled in 1958, by the tireless Schubert scholar Otto Erich Deutsch.*

BIOGRAPHICAL RECORDS

The memorials and notes contain many fascinating anecdotes and stories that afford a priceless glimpse of the living composer. But those written early after his death suffer from a serious unawareness of what Schubert had achieved in his life; and the later recollections, many written 30 or more years after the death, and at a time when Schubert's celebrity was more apparent,

---

* Deutsch, *Schubert: Memoirs by his Friends*.

often suffer from inaccurate recollection and a tendency to exaggerate the part played by the writer.

Among the earlier recollections of particular value are those written by his close and ever-loyal friend from school days Josef von Spaun, and by the poet and dramatist Eduard von Bauernfeld, one of whose poems had been set to music by Schubert (the two in fact worked together for a number of years at the National Lottery Administration). Their tributes were written in 1829, after the funeral and memorial events, but nothing further was recorded until Ferdinand and Franz Schubert senior wrote tributes to the composer which were included in a musical encyclopaedia published in 1838 by Gustav Schilling. A longer biographical sketch by Ferdinand was written at the request of Schumann and published in 1839 in the *Neue Zeitschrift für Musik*, of which he was the editor. Schumann had, of course, met Ferdinand on his famous visit in 1838 which had resulted in the dispatching of the *Great* C Major Symphony to Leipzig, from where it was to be rescued and revealed to the world.

FERDINAND LUIB

Another decade and more was to elapse before there were any further serious efforts to produce a proper biography of the dead composer. This was not entirely due to inactivity as the Austro-Hungarian Empire, together with most of mainland Europe, was convulsed by the revolutionary wars of 1848–49 which included the temporary siege of Vienna. It was, therefore, not till the 1850s that Franz Liszt began to pursue his scheme to produce a biography and catalogue of Schubert's works; and in parallel, in 1857, Ferdinand Luib, a Viennese music critic and former editor of *Allgemeine Wiener Musikzeitung*, independently took on the same task. Luib had been only 17 when Schubert died and had no personal knowledge of him. However, his interest in Schubert's music led to him collecting a list of Schubert's friends and acquaintances with whom he began systematically to correspond, collecting a considerable volume of material on the composer's life and works. This included a note from Eduard von Bauernfeld and a much enlarged piece from Josef von Spaun.

Luib's collection of responses, as now edited and published by Otto Erich Deutsch, while not further collated by Luib, contain some notable revelations. They include extensive responses from both the brothers Hüttenbrenner, which make interesting reading in the context of the *Unfinished* Symphony to which this chapter will shortly turn. When asked about original manuscripts, Anselm responds saying that he possessed Schubert's *Die Forelle*, and also *Die zürnende Diana* and *Gretchen am Spinnrade*. He adds that Schubert wrote 13 variations on a theme from Anselm's String Quartet and concluded: *'Finally, I am sending you two letters from Schubert.'* It is fair to ask how he came to overlook the manuscript of the *Unfinished* Symphony, which he had studied and worked on, as both brothers were fully aware. Josef, however, was unable to refrain from mentioning the work, and in a later note refers to the fact that Schubert dedicated 'a *Symphony in B Minor*' to Anselm which is not completed but *'can hold its own with any of Beethoven's.'** At the time (1858), no-one sought to follow this up, but it seems that Josef had made up his mind that the world should be told about the unknown work.

Sadly, Luib never completed the task of writing the biography and did not pursue the revelations which the memoirs had thrown up. It is not clear why he gave up the task, though Luib was known to be working on a biography of Beethoven at the same time. He was also aware that his work overlapped with that of the next biographer, who was to be the first to succeed in the task.

Dr Heinrich Kreissle von Hellborn had embarked on the same task as Luib and succeeded in producing an early draft of

---

* *Ibid.*, p. 76.

the biography in 1861, which was seen by Luib. As a result Luib decided to hand over his material to von Hellborn, who incorporated much of it in the final product (although with little acknowledgement), which was published some four years later. Von Hellborn was a Viennese lawyer, keen amateur musician and board member of the Gesellschaft der Musikfreunde. By the time he completed his research and published the full biography in 1865, Luib had died.

VON HELLBORN'S *LIFE OF FRANZ SCHUBERT*

Finally published in a single volume in German in 1865 – and, as we shall see, translated into English and published in two volumes in 1869 – the biography launched a new wave of interest in the composer in Austria, Germany and England. After reviewing Schubert's family circumstances up to 1813, it takes the life and compositions year by year from 1814 to the final year when Schubert's powers were, appropriately, said to be at their zenith. Much of the text is occupied with correspondence of which von Hellborn had acquired copies, and quotations from the tributes and recollections that had been solicited both by the author and by Ferdinand Luib. The text can be seen to reinforce (and to an extent even to originate) the notions that Schubert was poorly educated (*'wanting in what we call the higher branches of education'*), that he exhibited a *'characteristic wilfulness and obstinacy,'* was over-fond of drink which often left him inebriated, but had the good fortune to have friends (Franz von Schober, the poet Johann Mayrhofer, Vogl and others) who *'must have had an enduring intellectual influence over his thoughts and character.'* The self-serving testimony from which such conclusions were drawn can well be imagined. At least it stops short of suggesting that his worthy friends influenced his music. The description is more than somewhat at odds with the personal descriptions of the composer in later biographies; and indeed with the accounts of Schubert's most reliable companions, especially his constant friend Josef von Spaun. However, it is generally accepted that there was a darker side to Schubert's personality, of which much is heard in later biographies.*

The work includes extensive reviews of Schubert's music where von Hellborn quotes other authorities, especially Robert Schumann, but does not hesitate to add his own assessments, which are sometimes in accord with modern assessment and on occasions wildly at variance. Perhaps of greatest interest in the work today is the assembled list, as then known, of Schubert's compositions, comprising: the published and unpublished *lieder* (then numbering almost 600) together with part songs, cantatas, psalms, hymns and oratorios, pianoforte solos and duet compositions, chamber music, compositions for orchestra, operas, operettas, melodramas and church music. The latter included works attributed to Franz but at this stage were said to be written by Ferdinand (where modern scholarship has generally drawn the reverse conclusion).

When dealing with the operas, today the least known of all Schubert's output, the librettos are, surprisingly, quoted extensively – surprising because the author cannot have heard performances of most if any of the works. In the years preceding the biography, there had been a number of public performances of overtures and numbers from the operas. In October 1861 there had been a full performance of the *Die Verschworenen* (D787), a *Singspiel* based on *Lysistrata*, which the author could have attended. The text creates the impression, which Schubert himself would have welcomed, that the operas were a major element in the growing popularity of his music. That time is yet to arrive.

Von Hellborn's biography, while naturally eclipsed by the large volume of subsequent scholarship and writing on the composer's life and music was, despite its faults, a major milestone which spawned an outflow of further writing, particularly

---

* Particularly Elizabeth Norman McKay, *Franz Schubert: A Biography*, 1996.

in the German-speaking world, but significantly also in France* and England.† The list of compositions also represented an important advance in revealing the true extent of the achievements of a man who was at last being recognised as one of the greatest composers of his era.

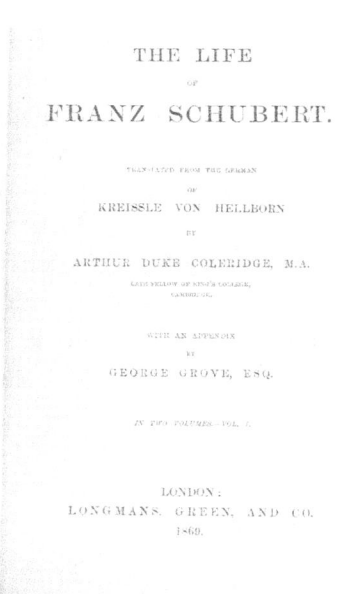

The English translation of von Hellborn's biography, published in two volumes in 1869

Whilst the von Hellborn biography is, rightly, listed by Deutsch as the first of the *'most important books on Schubert,'*‡ a work published in France by Hippolyte Barbedette very shortly after von Hellborn's biography, is not. The author dedicates this work to Albert Sowinski: *'Mon excellent ami,'* whose connection to Schubert was to have played the piano at a house concert held on 18 January 1827, which included a performance of *Sehnsucht*

---

* Hippolyte Barbedette, *Fr Schubert: Sa Vie, Ses Œuvres, Son Temps*, 1865.
† Grove, *Life of Schubert* in *Dictionary of Music and Musicians*, 1882.
‡ Deutsch, *Docs* p 962.

(it is not clear which version). Sowinski and the composer were certainly acquainted, since in April of the same year Schubert was to inscribe in Sowinski's journal the fourth and last autograph copy of *An die Musik*, a facsimile of which is included in the front of Barbedette's book.*

As regards the author, Hippolyte Barbedette, he had apparently read von Hellborn's shorter draft published in 1861, and in 1865, the same year as publication of the main work, produced an even shorter biography, which was largely drawn from von Hellborn's earlier work and contained little new material other than some letters and documents which von Hellborn had omitted. However the author does take the opportunity to add some comments on the last three piano sonatas where, having noted Schumann's poor opinion of the works, adds that (in his view) the sonatas present a *'naiveté d'invention'* and that *'ces sonates sont-elles d'une longueur fatigante,'* perhaps having overlooked Schumann's 'heavenly length.'†

The second 'most important book' listed by Deutsch is August Reissmann's *Life and Works of Schubert*, to which we will return in Chapter 10.

A NEW SYMPHONY

The von Hellborn biography also revealed, in what seemed to be a mere diversion, that there existed a hitherto unknown symphony which had been written by Schubert in 1822 and presented by him to the Graz musical society. The revelation came about in the following terms:

> An orchestral Symphony in B Minor, which Schubert presented, in a half finished state, to the Musikverein at Graz, in return for the compliment paid to him of being elected a honorary member

---

* Deutsch: *Docs* p 595, 634 and 699.
† *Ibid.*, p 68.

of that society. Josef Hüttenbrenner is my authority for saying that the first and second movements are entirely finished and the third (Scherzo) partly. The fragment in the possession of Herr Anselm Hüttenbrenner ... .*

The story of how the work originally came into the possession of the Hüttenbrenners has been set out earlier.† Suffice to say that Josef, as the go-between in the transaction, was well aware that his elder brother and budding composer in his own right, had not delivered the manuscript to the musical society but kept it, himself making a piano duet arrangement of the work in 1853, the importance of which he clearly realised. Josef had been a contemporary of Schubert and had done much to promote his music in the early years, but was also aware of the ambitions of his elder brother Anselm. Josef was active in arranging the memorial service after Franz's death and organised the music which, surprising to us now knowing the extent of Schubert's music for the church, included a mass by Anselm but none by Schubert.

Josef, by that time in poor health, had in fact written to the conductor Johann Herbeck in 1860 referring to the missing manuscript, but the letter was not then followed up. Now with the added reference in the biography, Herbeck was determined to find the work, if it existed. He therefore travelled to Graz and confronted Anselm, who finally agreed to surrender the manuscript on condition that the concert in which the symphony was to be given would also include music of his. So it was that on 17 December 1865, just months after the biography appeared, the *Unfinished* Symphony was performed for the first time, and fittingly in Vienna. The work was an instant success and further

---

* Von Hellborn, *Life of Franz Schubert*, v1 p 257 of the English edition. In the Appendix to the English edition, v11, p 317, Grove describes and quotes from the manuscript, then 'in the hands of Mr Herbeck, who was kind enough to show it to us.'
† See Chapter 2.

performances followed in many other venues. The newly discovered work proved a major turning point in the public's appreciation of Schubert's orchestral music which had been sorely lacking up to that point.

THE HÜTTENBRENNERS

There is no escaping the conclusion that both Anselm and Josef regarded Schubert as a serious rival to Anselm's ambitions, and one that would leave his own works in the shade. Unlike Salieri in the case of Mozart, there is no hint that the Hüttenbrenners were in any way complicit in Schubert's early death; but there is a strong likelihood that Anselm was intending, once the memories of Schubert had faded, to pass off the *Unfinished* Symphony as his own. That intention was to be defeated both by the continued interest in Schubert and his works, and then by his brother's indiscreet revelation of the symphony's existence. We should at least be grateful to Anselm for preserving the manuscript with such care. Fittingly, while Anselm Hüttenbrenner was regarded as a talented and serious composer in the first half of the nineteenth century, his main claim today to emerge from the obscurity which he richly deserves, is the set of piano variations written by Schubert (D576) on a not-very-inspiring theme from a String Quartet by his supposed friend.

The 1860s had therefore brought about two significant strides towards the acceptance of Franz Schubert as one of the greatest composers of his age: a systematic and thorough, if not wholly reliable, biography, including a catalogue of the works then known; and a new symphony of such beauty and originality as to convert the unconverted. And these strides were accompanied by the gradual but steady acceptance of other major works, including the late quartets and String Quintet, the piano trios and the *Great* C Major Symphony, as part of the standard concert repertoire across much of Europe including, as we shall see, England.

CHAPTER 9
AND DID THOSE FEET …

During and shortly after his lifetime, Schubert's music had spread into greater Germany, particularly Leipzig; and the *lieder* had certainly been taken up enthusiastically in France from the 1830s. However, while England had in the past been host to many famous musicians, there was no indication that Schubert's music had made any impression, at least up to 1850. But the situation was about to change.

VON HELLBORN TRANSLATED

In 1869, as an indication of the interest in the composer which was then gathering pace, von Hellborn's biography was translated into English by Arthur Duke Coleridge, the founder of the English Bach Choir. The translator's preface gives us a vivid picture of the transformation that was occurring in the perception of the composer in England. He states:

> It is scarcely an exaggeration to say that Schubert's reputation in England, until very recently, rested upon little more than half-a-dozen songs. We are now beginning to realise the importance of

his music; and if (as many believe) a great future be in store for Schubert in this country, let us acknowledge our obligations to the joint exertions of my friend Mr George Grove, and that admirable musician Mr Manns, conductor of the Crystal Palace concerts.

Coleridge might have added for completeness that Augustus Manns had already, in 1856, performed the *Great* C Major Symphony at the Crystal Palace.

England had a reputation, at least in the German-speaking world, as '*das Land ohne Musik.*' However unjustified that may seem to the descendants of Byrd, Tallis and Henry Purcell, England had not produced a composer of true stature during the first half of the nineteenth century, and in the previous one had relied largely on the imported talents of George Frideric Handel. By the end of the eighteenth century and into the nineteenth, there was an increasing demand for the best in European music, but it had been filled by imported stars including Joseph Haydn and later Felix Mendelssohn. So it was unsurprising that in the middle years of the century England, probably then the most prosperous country in the world, should again benefit from the services of two outstanding German musicians who were to play a pivotal role at the time Schubert's music was beginning to be heard.

MANNS AND HALLÉ

Augustus Manns, identified by Mr Coleridge, was a German-born conductor who, after serving as a military bandmaster, had chosen to pursue a musical career in England. He was appointed director of music at London's Crystal Palace in 1855, following its relocation after having housed the Great Exhibition of 1851 in Hyde Park. He increased the resident band to full symphonic strength and, within months of his appointment, gave the first London performances of Schumann's Symphony No 4 and the

British premiere of Schubert's *Great* C Major Symphony, which Mendelssohn had failed to persuade the London Philharmonic Orchestra to play in 1844.

Sir Augustus Manns

For the next 40 years Manns was the stalwart of music in Britain, along with his compatriot Charles Hallé, and enthusiastically supported by the secretary of the Crystal Palace Company, George Grove. Manns supported many younger musicians including Arthur Sullivan who, through Manns, was to become the famous travelling companion of Grove on his visit to Vienna. Manns became a British citizen in 1894 and was knighted for services to music in 1903.

The second German émigré, Charles Hallé, had studied the piano in Darmstadt and subsequently in Paris, where he associated with Chopin, Berlioz and Liszt. He also took the opportunity to adopt a French version of his name, formerly Halle, and continued to make use of it in his subsequent travels. He was forced to leave Paris as a result of the 1848 revolution and settled first in London and later in Manchester, where he both conducted and continued his career as a soloist. In this capacity he was the first to perform the complete Beethoven sonatas in England and the first to play nine of the Schubert sonatas, which were subsequently published In London.

Sir Charles Hallé

Later, in 1868, Hallé was to perform all 11 of Schubert's sonatas then in print. In Manchester, Hallé created the orchestra, still known as the Hallé, which performed at the Free Trade Hall and became the centre for musical performances in Manchester and the north of England. He also became a British citizen, was knighted and became a founder of the Royal Manchester College of Music, now the Royal Northern College of Music.

GEORGE GROVE

The third English celebrity, George Grove, was a native-born civil engineer and polymath who later gave his name to the

Grove Dictionary of Music and Musicians, originally published in 1878. In his capacity as secretary for the Crystal Palace concerts, Grove, with Manns, became an enthusiastic promoter of Schubert's music, which was then becoming available as publishers in Vienna put more works into circulation. Through the publisher C. A. Spina, as successor to Diabelli, Grove had obtained a series of numbers from the music for *Rosamunde* and some overtures, which had met with an enthusiastic response at the Crystal Palace concerts. News of the *Unfinished* Symphony also reached Grove after its rescue and performance by Herbeck at the end of 1865. Grove was able to obtain the score and put on the first performance at the Crystal Palace in April 1867. The work firmly established Schubert's appeal to the London audience and left Grove with a serious determination to find more of the same, particularly the missing parts of the *Rosamunde* music and other symphonies.

GROVE AND SULLIVAN IN VIENNA

Grove was able to fulfil this ambition in October 1867, accompanied by the young Arthur Sullivan (some years before the Savoy operas). The account of their visit to Vienna is found as an Appendix to Volume 2 of the English translation of von Hellborn's biography, the translation being published in 1869. Grove was confident that there was more to be discovered, and had been provided by the publisher Spina with an introduction to Dr Schneider, Schubert's nephew, who had acquired the contents of the famous chest on the death of Ferdinand in 1859. On arrival in Vienna, therefore, Grove and Sullivan attended upon Dr Schneider who obligingly made available the large collection of original manuscripts. These were found to contain the hitherto unknown Symphonies No 1–4 and 6. No 5, as will be seen, had a more colourful history and eventually found its way to Berlin, but not before Ferdinand had made the copy that Manns was later to perform in London.

Sir George Grove

It will be recalled that Ferdinand, despite serious efforts, had failed to attract any interest in either publishing or performing the symphonies, which had not been heard since Schubert's day. On this occasion the visitors expressed great interest and were allowed to take the symphonies away for closer inspection. Grove also paid a visit to the Gesellschaft der Musikfreunde, where he was shown the manuscript of the *Great* C Major Symphony, as it had been left by Schubert, bearing the date March 1828 and containing Schubert's numerous alterations to the original score. Grove was able to make a full note of the alterations and subsequently prepared the detailed account which is also found in the Appendix to Volume 2 of the English translation of the biography. The Appendix also contains notes on Symphonies No 1–4 and No 6, plus No 7 (the sketch as so described), which had been presented to Grove by the brother of Felix Mendelssohn, to whom it had been sent by Ferdinand; and No 8 (which had been published earlier in 1867) and other works including the sonata for Arpeggione ('whatever that may have been,' as Grove described it).

However, of the missing parts of the *Rosamunde* score there was no sign, until Grove was permitted himself to enter and search through the dusty cupboard in Dr Schneider's office. Here he finally discovered what he had most hoped for: the missing numbers and indeed the complete *Rosamunde* music, in its original orchestral parts. These had been neatly tied up after the final performance in December 1823 and had lain undisturbed, first in Ferdinand's chest and then in Dr Schneider's cupboard, for 44 years. With assistance, Grove and Sullivan were able to make copies of the missing numbers as well as of the symphonies. The visitors also witnessed the many other works of Schubert, both known and unknown, still awaiting publication. At the conclusion of his account of the visit, Grove adds: 'As for Schubert, his place in the world is certain.'

MUSIC IN ENGLAND

Returning to the 1830s and the following decade, there is little evidence of awareness of Schubert's works in England other than in an occasional performance of particularly celebrated *lieder* – *Erlkönig* was performed and published in an English translation in 1832. But, as Arthur Coleridge observed, up to the 1850s Schubert's reputation rested on half-a-dozen songs, which were performed usually by visiting soloists. Mendelssohn, after having failed to conduct the *Great* C Major Symphony in 1844, substituted a performance of the overture to *Fierrabras*, which was not well received and did not lead to further performances or any further demand for Schubert's music following Mendelssohn's tour. It was the advent of Charles Hallé which began the introduction of Schubert's chamber music to England, starting with the piano sonatas and Impromptus and then performing the piano trios in the 1850s at concerts in London, which also attracted international soloists including Clara Schumann. It must be remembered that, by 1850, rapid travel by rail was increasingly possible and one of the valuable commodities it was able to transport was music, and the artists who performed that music.

Among visiting artists in London in the 1850s and 1860s was the celebrated violinist Joseph Joachim (a close friend of Brahms), both as a soloist and subsequently with his quartet which performed Schubert's quartets and the now famous String Quintet. Other major chamber pieces were performed in the 1860s: the *Quartettsatz* (D703) was given in London in 1867 and the early String Trio in B flat (D581) in 1869. But in 1856 Manns had conducted the *Great* C Major Symphony at the Crystal Palace, given in two parts on 5 and 12 April; the first three movements being given at the first concert and the Andante, Scherzo and final movement at the second. It is reported that Grove had been persuaded to attend these performances and, as a result, became and remained an ardent supporter of Schubert's music.

FIRST PERFORMANCES

From this point on, Grove, together with Manns and Hallé, were actively promoting Schubert's orchestral music wherever they could. This culminated in Grove's visit to Vienna, after which, armed with the hitherto ignored early symphonies, the Crystal Palace was able to present the first performances in England, of Symphonies No 4 and No 6, both performed in 1868 and of No 5 in 1873. In 1877, Manns was to conduct the world premiere, in modern times, of Symphony No 2 and in 1881 the premieres of No 1 and No 3. To add to this glittering achievement, the premiere of a recently completed version of the sketched Symphony in E, still referred to as No 7, completed by J. F. Barnett, was performed in 1883. From the mid-1860s, as a result of the endeavours of Manns, Hallé and Grove, Schubert acquired an unprecedented popularity in England, which was maintained to the end of the century and beyond.

It should not be thought that the growing enthusiasm for Schubert was without a dissenting voice. In fact no lesser critic than George Bernard Shaw, celebrated playwright but amateur music critic, took a determined stand in opposition in his three volume *Music in London 1890–94*. Writing of the Crystal Palace concert series he noted that 'there is an understanding among regular frequenters that a performance of Schubert's Symphony in C is one of the specialities of the place … and Mr Manns always receives a special ovation at the end.' After some denigration of the work itself Shaw observed 'how much better than Schubert' was Rossini, whose centenary had recently passed. He also, strangely, labelled Schubert as a 'man with second class brains, however wonderful his musical endowments.'[*]

Where can Shaw have picked up the notion that Schubert was in some way intellectually lacking? With writings about Schubert's life still comparatively rare, it was likely that Shaw had informed himself through the works of von Hellborn and the subsequent contributions of Grove himself,[†] and concluded that Schubert lacked education and that his works, while possessing charm, lacked any depth. History has judged otherwise, especially with the advantage of knowledge rather than ill-informed guesswork. And Shaw's comparison with Rossini has, without denigrating the qualities of the Italian, been reversed by the progressive appreciation of the quality and craftsmanship to be discovered in the works of Schubert.

MORE ENGLISH SCHOLARS

The promotion and appreciation of Schubert's works in England continued into the twentieth century with increasing support from the musical public and a number of notable celebrities. Among the latter, England was fortunate that Otto Erich Deutsch, the compiler of the great collection of Schubert documents, originally published in Germany in 1914, took refuge in

---

[*] Vol II p 53.
[†] See chapter 10.

England in the 1930s to avoid the Nazi takeover in his native Vienna. He moved to Cambridge in 1939 where he was able to resume his scholarly activities producing (among publications on Handel and Mozart) his famous thematic catalogue of Schubert's works in English, in 1952, which was later translated into German. The great collection of documents (*The Schubert Reader: A Life of Franz Schubert in Letters and Documents*) was translated into English by Eric Blom in 1946. In 1957, Deutsch published an edited volume of the collected *Schubert: Memoirs by his Friends*, including those solicited by Luib and von Hellborn, which was translated into English in 1958. Deutsch without doubt inspired the next generation of English Schubert scholars, including Maurice Brown and John Reed, whose works have, in turn, firmly established the continuing tradition of English scholarship.

FRANCE

In contrast to the slow development of interest in Schubert's music in England, the reception in France was quite different. France had its own strong musical traditions, perhaps more so than England, and no shortage of celebrated composers resident in or performing in Paris, including Chopin and Liszt. However, despite the popular belief that it was the *lieder* which spread Schubert's reputation throughout Europe, it was Schubert's chamber music that first achieved a following in France.* By 1834 the E flat Piano Trio had been published together with four of the string quartets, including the D Minor and A Minor, and a number of piano compositions for both solo and four hands. By the mid 1830s the *lieder* were beginning to achieve popularity, albeit there was a demand for arrangements, following the trend set by Liszt. The leading performer of *lieder* in France at the time was the tenor Adolphe Nourrit, who himself is said to have been

---

* Xavier Hascher, *The Cambridge Companion to Schubert*, ed. Gibbs, 1997.

inspired by Liszt's performances. Nourrit became celebrated for his performances of *Le Roi des aulnes* (*Erlkönig*) and *La Jeune Religieuse* (*Die junge Nonne*), albeit popular in orchestral arrangements. But by 1850 the publisher C. S. Richault in Paris had published 367 of the *lieder* in 16 volumes, with French translations. One consequence was that Hector Berlioz made his orchestral arrangement of *Erlkönig*, which he generously credited to the inspiration of Nourrit. His arrangement is still heard today.

The orchestral works fared less well. The *Great* C Major Symphony was performed in full in 1851 but not well received and then not performed again until 1873. There was no rush, after its discovery in 1865, to perform the *Unfinished* Symphony, whose first movement was played only in 1878 and both movements had to wait until 1881. The prominent French critic François-Joseph Fétis considered Schubert's instrumental works to be less original than his songs, the popularity of which he considered to be largely a matter of fashion (Dvořák, in 1894, claimed this opinion was too absurd to call for comment). Nevertheless it is clear that the orchestral works were not received in France with anything approaching the enthusiasm of the Crystal Palace audiences in London. A biography in French was published in 1865,[*] which drew heavily on the first draft of the biography by von Hellborn. The centenary in 1928 saw the publication of a number of articles in French including a major study by Jacques-Gabriel Prod'homme,[†] which contains the only attempt at translating the documents collected by Deutsch into French. It is thus fair to say that, while Schubert was recognised early in France as a composer of the first rank and that his music has been performed widely although selectively, the French did not take the composer to heart in the way seen in England from the 1860s onwards.

It is perhaps ironic that, during the period of great alliances

---

[*] Barbedette, *Fr Schubert, Sa Vie, Ses Oeuvres, Son Temps*.
[†] Jacques-Gabriel Prod'homme, Schubert Raconté Par Ceux qui l'ont Vu.

and major conflicts between the European powers of France, Britain and the German-speaking world, a composer of genius from Austria should be received in Britain rather than France with such enthusiasm – a reception largely due to the influence of two distinguished German musicians who happened to choose England to pursue their careers. The key to his affinity, which continues today lies, of course, in the music which also inspired the tireless work of George Grove, the amateur whose enthusiasm opened a pathway to others who have established and continued the English tradition of Schubert scholarship.

PART III REVELATION

CHAPTER 10
THE 1870S AND BEYOND

By 1870 it can confidently be said that Schubert, and his music, were generally known and appreciated throughout Europe and elsewhere, including the United States. In this chapter we see some of the ways in which his growing celebrity was marked as his music continued to be performed and enjoyed. Much more was still to be revealed, but there was no longer any risk that he might be forgotten.

THE STADTPARK MEMORIAL

Despite the popularity of his music, there is only one public monument erected to commemorate the composer in Vienna, other than the bust commissioned for his grave at the Währing cemetery. The single monument is the life-size statue, seated on an imposing plinth, in the Stadtpark, which today is a familiar sight to tourists and a welcome reminder of the veneration which the Viennese, belatedly, bestowed on Schubert as their only major native composer.*

---

* Josef Haydn was of course a native Austrian and spent much of the later part of his life in Vienna.

The Schubert Denkmal

We left the statue in Chapter 6, at the point, in 1868, when sufficient funds had been raised for the foundation stone to be laid. However, the story is not quite as straightforward as suggested by these bare facts; there was a much deeper historical and political significance.

For centuries the Austro-Hungarian Empire had regarded itself as the leader of the greater Germany (although there was no such nation until 1871) and certainly the leader of German culture, despite only one third of the Austro-Hungarian Empire's population being German-speaking. During the nineteenth century, particularly after the demise of Napoleon, this leadership was seriously challenged by Prussia to the extent that a war broke out in 1866, ending in the humiliating defeat of Austria at the Battle of Königgrätz. By 1868 German-speaking Vienna, therefore, welcomed the opportunity to re-establish Austrian domination of German *lieder* through a demonstration of renewed veneration of their great home-grown composer, and expressed through that most German medium, the male-voice choir.

The monument was completed and unveiled in May 1872, bearing an inscription which records the support of the Männergesang-Verein. It also benefitted from substantial moral as well as financial support from Nikolaus Dumba, the great Schubertian and philanthropist. Now known as the Schubert Denkmal, it occupied a prominent position in the Stadtpark on the newly created Vienna Ring (Ringstrasse), opposite the Dumba mansion, no doubt also recognising the Dumba contribution to the project. The mansion was famously adorned with paintings, including the celebrated depiction by Gustav Klimt of Schubert seated at the piano, which was sadly destroyed in the Second World War but known today from photographs and copies. The section of the Ring in which the statue is located was originally named the Kolowratring but as part of the centenary tributes of 1928 was renamed the Schubertring.

It remains ironic that, while male-voice part songs were one of Schubert's popular fields of composition during and for some decades after his lifetime, the genre has seriously declined in popularity, except in Vienna, where the society continues to flourish. There are, in fact, two male voice choirs in Vienna, the more recent, founded in 1863, being the Lehrersängerchor Schubertbund, or simply the Schubertbund, which is dedicated to performing the works of Schubert. While the part songs are today less often heard, they were enthusiastically performed at the unveiling ceremony for which Herbeck also conducted a performance of the recently rediscovered *Unfinished* Symphony, and the Hellmesberger Quartet performed the Adagio from the String Quintet. It is of some interest that the ethereal Adagio of the quintet, as well as the *Unfinished* Symphony, which are today regarded as two of the pinnacles of Schubert's art, were even then recognised as fitting accompaniments to the final unveiling.

Schubert at the Piano by Gustav Klimt

A SECOND MAJOR BIOGRAPHY

The publication of von Hellborn's biography in 1865 led, partly aided by the advent of the *Unfinished* Symphony, to a resurgence of publishing activity. This was particularly so in Leipzig, where *lieder* and chamber works were republished and piano transcriptions, including four-hand arrangements of the early symphonies, became popular. There were also further biographies and treatises on Schubert's music in German, notably a study by August Reissmann published in 1873: *Franz Schubert, Sein Leben und Seine Werke*. Reissman was a native of Silesia and, as well as being an accomplished musician, became a prolific writer on music and musicians, publishing biographies of Schumann (1865), Mendelssohn (1867), Schubert (1873) and Haydn (1879). The study of Schubert is a worthy and necessary sequel to von Hellborn's account of the life and works, which contained little analysis of the music or of Schubert's place in the development of music in the nineteenth century. Reissmann was able to present a comparison of Schubert's position with that of Schumann and Mendelssohn and concluded that whilst these composers were caught up in the new world of romanticism, Schubert was able to compose with greater freedom. Reissmann had access to more of Schubert's unpublished works through the publisher Spina and noted the significance of Schubert's dance music, which had elevated the genre and led to its greatly enhanced popularity.

From the 1870s onwards, therefore, Schubert was well established in the German-speaking world and, as we have seen, also in England and in France, as a major composer. In each country there was growing interest in his works, which continued to be performed regularly, despite there being different preferences and fashions in different countries. And Schubert's music continued to hold its own despite a vast body of new music being written by composers including Wagner, Brahms and Tchaikovsky. That Schubert's reputation was now secure is shown most clearly by the perseverance of the musical authorities in Austria and Germany towards creating a complete edition of his works, which would finally commence in earnest in 1884 (the subject of Chapter 11), and by the memorials erected in his honour.

GROVE'S SECOND VISIT

Grove paid a further visit to Vienna in 1880 where he collected more material on the composer which he published, in 1882, in what became a classic work in the English language: *The Life of Schubert*, contained in what was to become *Grove's Dictionary of Music and Musicians*. This was a significant further advance in the spread of knowledge of the composer and his music in England. However, Grove's account of the life shows the continuing influence of the original biography of von Hellborn, which was based on often misleading and self-serving accounts written by those claiming intimate knowledge of Schubert. The degree of misinformation concerning Schubert's musical education still pervading Grove's account is shown by the following extract:

> Had but a portion of the pains been spent on the musical education of Schubert that was lavished on that of Mozart or of Mendelssohn, we can hardly doubt that even his transcendent ability would have been enhanced by it, that he would have gained that control over the prodigious spontaneity of his genius which is his only want, and have risen to the very highest level in all departments of composition, as he did in songwriting.

And of Schubert's personal life Grove writes:

> Good God, it makes one's blood boil to think of so fine and rare a genius, one of the ten or twelve topmost men in the world, in want of even the common necessaries of life. Failure, disappointment, depreciation, and suchlike shocks and wounds of the heart and soul, these are the necessary accompaniments of a fine intellect and a sensitive heart; but to want the ordinary comforts and amenities of life, to want bread, it is too dreadful to think of.

These largely fictitious passages helped to perpetuate a series of myths about Schubert which persisted through the nineteenth century and well into the twentieth. Perhaps most pernicious is the suggestion, which originated with friends and colleagues who did know Schubert well, that his musical compositions were the result of 'somnambulism' or divine dictation. Even Johann Michael Vogl entertained such a belief which has persisted due to the supposed absence of drafts or notes of the works, which were then known only as finished manuscripts. The notion has been thoroughly debunked by the discovery of working drafts for many works. But it remains the case that the fluency and rapidity of many of Schubert's compositions is difficult to believe. And a proper appreciation of the true measure of his genius is far from universal. At least the implication in Grove's account that, with a proper education Schubert might have achieved even more – no doubt meaning a closer adherence to the great model of Beethoven – can now be confidently dismissed.

THE ZENTRALFRIEDHOF MEMORIAL

We have seen that the first and more modest memorial to the composer, installed for the original grave at the Währing cemetery, consisted of a bronze bust of Schubert for which funds had been raised at two memorial concerts in 1829. The grave is surmounted by a dignified plinth containing the bust. The graveyard is now closed and the area renamed Schubert Park. However, for Schubert's grave, it is necessary to look further.

Schubert, as he had wished, was buried close to the grave of Beethoven, who had been interred in the newly opened Währing cemetery in 1827, after a funeral procession in which Schubert was one of the mourners. In 1863 the Vienna authorities, now mindful of the celebrity of the two composers buried at Währing, decided to repair the site and arranged for the bodies to be disinterred and placed in new metal coffins. The new coffins were reinterred at Währing but this again proved to be a temporary arrangement. During the 1860s, burial grounds around the old city had become overcrowded and the municipality decided to embark on a project to build, some way out from the centre, the new Zentralfriedhof, a massive new cemetery to serve the whole city. However, it appears its relatively remote location made it unpopular so the authorities decided to seek other ways to make it more attractive. For this reason, and perhaps also as an expression of Austrian national pride, the decision was taken that the great and good of Vienna's past should now be reinterred in the Zentralfriedhof in what is called the *Ehrengräber* section, or honorary graves. These would be located in different sections of the cemetery dedicated to various fields of distinction, one of these being music.

Schubert's new grave in the Zentralfriedhof

So it was that in 1888 two of the city's greatest sons were reinterred here, from the modest burial ground at Währing. As Schubert had wished, he and Beethoven were to be reinterred together; and to complete the picture the authorities decided to add a memorial to Mozart who had, of course, been buried in an unmarked pauper's grave almost a century earlier. It is recorded that before the final reinterring the coffins were to be reopened. Hearing of what was intended, Anton Bruckner, who was well-known for his fascination with corpses, booked a ringside seat and was reported to have fingered and kissed the skulls of both composers, one hopes in homage to their artistry.

Thus a second major memorial to Schubert was erected, in the company of his fellow composers: the Mozart memorial in the centre, Beethoven on the left and Schubert on the right, an arrangement which most today would commend as entirely fitting.

The account, up to this point, has shown how it came about that Franz Schubert, who had died in relative obscurity 60 years earlier was, by 1888, seen as worthy of the company of Mozart and Beethoven and how Viennese taste had changed so radically in the six decades that had elapsed since his death. The journey had not been a smooth progression and at times it seemed his memory would fade into obscurity. But what shines through the difficult times is the certainty that there will always be a body of devotees who, having been once inspired by his music, will apply their energy to furthering his cause and spreading his reputation ever wider; the body of supporters who can now be called the Schubertians.

CHAPTER 11
COLLECTING THE WORKS

The task of creating a catalogue of the works left to us by Schubert at his early death is essential to an appreciation of the music, both in terms of discovering what the composer composed but also when, in terms of dates and in relation to other works. In Schubert's case both tasks have proved to be immense, having been started in the 1830s but then continuing as different individuals were motivated to assist. The story runs in parallel with the slow but gradual promotion of Schubert as one of the world's truly great composers.

COLLATING THE MANUSCRIPTS

Schubert was perhaps the most prolific composer of all time and seems to have taken little regard for the manuscripts once completed. Many were left with friends and colleagues, others with publishers, and major pieces including full opera scores were sent off in the hope of securing a performance and then seemingly forgotten by the composer. In this era of digital reproduction it must be remembered that every work Schubert composed was as a single, unique manuscript. Some, especially the popular songs, were copied, often many times, but of the great bulk of his work, no copies existed unless and until they were published. At his unexpected death, his life's work lay scattered, mostly as individual manuscripts, throughout Vienna and further afield within Austria.

A number of friends and admirers had already made collections and copies of manuscripts, particularly the *lieder*. The task of collecting the works together after his death was initially undertaken by Ferdinand as we have seen. But there was another related and important aspect of the task, in collating and listing the manuscripts and seeking to organise them into an order with dates of composition. Only by these means could it be discovered what the dead composer had left to the world. The task would take the rest of the nineteenth century and is hardly complete today.

There are two separate projects, which have been ongoing in a variety of ways since the time of Schubert's death. The first is a thematic catalogue of all the works and their different movements or sections; the second is the physical (and now electronic) collection and publication of all his compositions. The projects overlap in many respects and have a common objective of creating a full account of the works composed, but they are essentially different in character and have been undertaken by different compilers and researchers over many years. Their detailed implementation has also changed as methods of publication and copying have evolved. In fact a thematic catalogue was the first to be achieved, but was necessarily preceded by lists of the collected works.

THE COLLECTED WORKS

Schubert, unlike Mozart and Beethoven, kept no journal or list of compositions but simply dated the manuscripts when completed. This has provided a mine of information but has also raised many problems for researchers. During Schubert's lifetime and for some decades afterwards, the composer's own dates were largely ignored in favour of opus numbers which gave only the date of publication. Lists of opus numbers were drawn up by the publishers, particularly Diabelli, who made lists of works up to Opus 74 and then 87, both in 1827. After the composer's death, which saw the publication of *lieder* accelerate, a further list was created in 1831 up to Opus 131, with other publishers producing their own lists, all with the laudable objective of promoting sales. However, as part of his memorial article of 1829, Eduard von Bauernfeld produced a short chronological list of Schubert's major works, the first of its kind. This was followed in 1835 by Ferdinand's list of the known works in chronological order, which was intended to promote or encourage performances, and which even reached Schumann in Leipzig. And as the publishers continued with the backlog of *lieder* and piano works they had purchased, lists of the works which had been published were also produced, including an early version of the thematic catalogue, drawn up by Diabelli in 1851.

The idea of a comprehensive collection of the works continued to gain support and in 1865 the publisher Spina, as successor to Diabelli, was engaged in planning a complete edition of the works. There were plans for separate editions of the *lieder* and of the piano works, but these were somewhat eclipsed by the publication, also in 1865, of what was intended as a comprehensive list of the composer's works in the first biography, *The Life of Franz Schubert* by Heinrich Kreissle von Hellborn. This inhibited neither the creation of other lists of works nor further biographies, but the size of the task of compiling a comprehensive collection of the works grew as the true volume of the material to be published became more apparent, as did the magnitude of the task of editing the works.

THE *GESAMTAUSGABE*

During the 1880s the list of authorities involved in collecting and collating the works, then almost exclusively Austrian and

German individuals, was joined by the notable English Schubertian Sir George Grove, whose journey to Vienna in 1867 has already been described. Grove published a list of Schubert's works in his *Dictionary of Music and Musicians* in 1883. By this date a committee was in the process of being created by the Leipzig publisher Breitkopf & Härtel, originally instigated and financed by the major Schubert collector and enthusiast Nikolaus Dumba, to undertake the creation and publication of the *Complete and Authoritative Edition* of Schubert's works.

The collected edition, otherwise referred to as the *Gesamtausgabe*, began to appear in 1884. Thereafter, it continued as different types of composition were progressively researched up to 1897, eventually filling 22 series in 39 folio volumes, of some 10,000 pages in all. There were eight editors of the specialised series including Josef Hellmesberger, with Johannes Brahms acting as chairman as well as editing the symphonies, and the musicologist Eusebius Mandyczewski as general secretary. Mandyczewski took on the enormous task of editing the 10 volumes of the *lieder*.

The *Gesamtausgabe* remained the definitive edition of the complete works for some six decades and was reprinted from 1965 by Dover Publications. From 1963 a *New Schubert Edition* (*Neue Schubert-Ausgabe*), was commissioned, to be published from 1979 by Bärenreiter (Kassel) in 83 volumes and eight series. The edition is now available online and is accompanied by critical commentaries, published separately by the International Schubert Society, and held in libraries throughout Europe, including the British Library in London, as well as Tokyo and Washington, DC.

To anyone who has seen and handled the full array of volumes of the *Gesamtausgabe* there is an overwhelming feeling of astonishment that any person could have composed such a volume of music, least of all a man who died before his 32nd birthday. The next impression on delving into the volumes is how much music there remains that is infrequently if ever heard. Schubert remains an enigma.

THEMATIC CATALOGUE

The need for a thematic catalogue, recording the opening notes of each individual work, is clear to anyone familiar with the huge range of the music. But such a catalogue must start with the listing of works to be recorded. As we have seen, a number of such lists were compiled initially during Schubert's lifetime by publishers, and subsequently by many others including Ferdinand as part of his attempts to sell, or at least to put the works into circulation. However, the first attempt to add themes to the lists of works was undertaken by Aloys Fuchs, a near contemporary of Schubert who had participated in Schubertiads and put together a substantial collection of the manuscripts. He compiled his catalogue in 1845, which was added to by Ferdinand and further enlarged by Josef Wilhelm Witteczek, another contemporary to whom Schubert had dedicated a number of *lieder*. They were able to draw on the earlier work of Karl Pinterics, who had been a major collector of Schubert *lieder*.

Then in 1851 the publisher Diabelli, still in the process of publishing the great collection of *lieder* purchased from Ferdinand, produced a substantial thematic catalogue of Schubert's published works including those which had appeared posthumously up to Opus 160. And finally, in the nineteenth century at least, the successor to Diabelli's publishing house, C. A. Spina, in 1874 commissioned and published a comprehensive thematic catalogue, prepared by Gustav Nottebohm, a Viennese pianist and teacher whose studies in Leipzig in the 1840s had brought him into contact with Mendelssohn and Schumann. His pupils included Eusebius Mandyczewski who, as we have seen, was to play a major role in the collected works.

Nottebohm had expertise in preparing a thematic catalogue of Beethoven's compositions and was able to draw together the accumulating knowledge of the works of Schubert into a comprehensive thematic catalogue. The result, *Thematisches Verzeichnis der im Druck erschienenen Werke von Franz Schubert*, would remain the standard authoritative work up to the mid-twentieth century. However, all the catalogues up to this point had suffered from being based substantially on the sequence of publishing and opus numbers, and thus bore little relation to the true order of composition. The task of producing a proper chronological thematic catalogue awaited a new scholar.

Nottebohm's catalogue was finally superseded by the Austrian scholar and authority on Schubert's works, O. E. Deutsch, who was the first to produce a full thematic catalogue. This was prepared in England during the 1940s and in English, but not published, largely due to wartime restrictions, until 1952. It was later republished in German with an enlarged edition in 1978. Deutsch's catalogue finally arranged the works in their order of composition, as revealed by various means, including the dates the composer frequently recorded on the manuscript and in many cases by analysis of contemporary records. This has naturally given rise to many issues as to the dates so assigned, some of which are now generally accepted as inaccurate. Deutsch's lasting achievement, however, was that he was able, following the precedent of Köchel with Mozart, to assign to each work its own 'D' (Deutsch) number, by which the work may be uniquely referred to.

Though opus numbers remain in use, they reveal nothing but the order of publication and D numbers are now universally adopted. In some ways it is strange that the thematic catalogue published originally in the 1870s should have preceded the comprehensive listing of the works. The reason is simply the almost overwhelming volume of work which Schubert left behind at his death. Despite his short life he was simply the most prolific of all composers, as the sight of his collected and published works will readily confirm. As we shall see, Schubert's compositions included 6 full masses plus a host of separate sacred works, 18 stage works including musical plays, many of which were unfinished, 7 completed and many partly completed symphonies, 13 completed and many partly completed solo piano sonatas. To this array we need to add over 600 *lieder*, a large number of chamber works, including piano duets, and a large volume of part songs, before turning to his most popular works, the piano Impromptus, Moments Musicaux and other pieces. The list is indeed formidable.

Without in any way diminishing the quality of Deutsch's scholarship, one of the most serious mis-attributions, now plain to contemporary readers, is the incorrect assignment of the *Great* C Major Symphony to 1828 (as Schubert himself had dated the manuscript) and consequently giving the work the D number 944. Deutsch was a firm believer in the lost Gastein Symphony of 1825 to which he assigns the separate D number 849 and adds, in the entry for the Grand Duo for piano duet in C Major, D812, that this work was thought to be the piano score of the lost symphony.

After more than a century following Schubert's death, the musical world was at last provided with the full published collection of the works and a catalogue of the music in chronological order. We are thus finally able to grasp the effective stages of Schubert's composing career, and to understand more clearly the relationships of the works and the progress of the composer's life.

CHAPTER 12
THE CENTENARY – A CHANCE TO REFLECT

There were, of course, two centenaries – the first to commemorate Schubert's birth in 1797, and the second to mark his untimely death in 1828. The fact that the first centenary was widely anticipated and planned for is itself a mark of the progress achieved by the many individuals who devoted themselves to promoting his music in earlier decades. We have seen that by the 1890s, the publication of the full collected works was well underway as the centenary of Schubert's birth approached. The publication of the complete works was achieved initially in 1894 but, as was to happen on other occasions, more original works came to light and a 'final' additional volume, No 39, was published for the centenary.

The anniversary was marked, particularly in Vienna, by the continued celebration of the city's own native composer, following the inauguration of the Denkmal. The Viennese, like much of Europe, had an excellent postal service which was used for the exchange of personal messages via postcards, many of them featuring popular Schubert themes. The centenary of 1897 was also marked by the musical world through festivals and performances on an international scale. In Vienna, there were 10 days of concerts, and Emperor Franz Joseph gave a speech recognising Schubert as the creator of the art song, and one of Austria's favourite sons. The city of Vienna arranged a Schubert exhibition in the Künstlerhaus. Karlsruhe saw the first production of the opera *Fierrabras*. Although somewhat late in the day, the Vienna city authorities at last purchased the building which housed the small apartment in which Franz had been born and raised for the first few years of his life. The apartment itself, although still in its original form, was extended to create a museum which now houses various original items of furniture including a contemporary piano. The museum also has the original bust from the grave at Währing cemetery, a pair of Schubert's own spectacles (one lens cracked) and many other exhibits.

TWO CENTENARIES

Then, with the passage of just 31 years, measuring out the composer's own lifespan, the next centenary of Schubert's death in 1828, came round. Although the world, and Austria in particular, was still recovering from the shock of the First World War, the third week of November 1928 was designated Schubert Week and was celebrated across Europe and in the United States. To mark the centenary, Schubert's works were performed in churches, in concert halls, and now on radio stations in different countries. And the exchange of postcards continued.

Again, Vienna led the celebrations but the event was now more of an international festival. Austria had, of course, by 1928 as a consequence of its defeat in the First World War, lost its huge former empire and been reduced in size to a rump of its former territories.

Many new books were published and tributes recorded for the anniversary. One of the books was produced by the English writer Newman Flower who, as well as researching the Luib documents, had the rare distinction of being conducted to the Schubert haunts in Vienna (then, of course, a mere 100 years after Schubert's last visit) by the great Schubert authority Professor Otto Erich Deutsch. The interest in this tour is that, as recorded in the second edition of the book in 1949, some of these locations had by that date been destroyed in the course of the Second World War. Flower not only wrote books on a number of composers but took over and transformed the publishing house Cassell & Co and was knighted for his services.

Commemorative card for 1928

This was the era of the gramophone and as its tribute to Schubert, no doubt also with an eye to sales, Columbia Records organised, jointly with the Gesellschaft der Musikfreunde in Vienna, an international competition for a completion of the *Unfinished* Symphony (D759). It was open to composers throughout the world, with a jury of distinguished musicians and musicologists, including Carl Nielsen and Donald Tovey, and chaired by the Russian composer Alexander Glazunov. The competition rules also permitted original works to be submitted and in the result the jury was more impressed with these than with the *Unfinished* Symphony completions.

However the seed had been sown and the attempts to

complete the B Minor Symphony would continue, and indeed continue to this day. The 1928 competition was in any event supported by a surge of new recordings of Schubert's music issued by Columbia, which were accompanied by a commemorative booklet containing a tribute to the composer by Alexander Glazunov entitled *Side by Side with Beethoven*. In this he remarks on the influence of Schubert on Russian music through Glinka and particularly through Borodin, whose music was said to carry the imprint of Schubert as his great precursor.

SCHUBERT'S PLACE AFTER A CENTURY

What had been achieved by the increasing number of enlightened Schubert enthusiasts in the century following his birth and the century following his death? First it can be said, with confidence, that Schubert had been elevated from the status of a popular composer of *lieder* in Vienna but virtually unknown elsewhere, to that of an internationally acknowledged master who was now to be seen alongside other nineteenth-century composers who had rightly achieved celebrity in their own lifetime, a recognition denied to Schubert.

The lack of recognition during Schubert's lifetime can be seen as the underlying cause of the extraordinary accumulation of unpublished and largely unperformed manuscripts that were left at his death and which could, but for the loyal exertions of brother Ferdinand, have been lost or destroyed. It is noticeable that Haslinger had agreed with Ferdinand for the purchase of the *Schwanengesang lieder* within a month of the death, whereas the more cautious Diabelli did not tie up the deal to purchase the much larger consignment of manuscripts until early 1830 – a decision indicative of understandable commercial caution and doubt as to the enduring celebrity of the now dead composer.

There had, in fact, been a surge of publications in the two years following Schubert's death in 1828, with some 50 new works being published, the majority being *lieder*, part songs or cantatas but also solo and four-hand piano works and chamber compositions including the *Trout* Quintet (Opus 114, D667). Thereafter there were gaps in the sequence of publications suggestive of an element of further caution or 'wait and see.' This was then broken by more modest surges in publications in 1837–1840 and in 1846–1849 and then a further group of chamber works in 1850–1853, to include, finally, the String Quintet following its first performance. The final surge in 1863–1865 of some 15 new works was probably the result of renewed interest associated with the appearance of von Hellborn's biography.

What emerges, understandably, is that the path to recognition was far from smooth and the process was moved forward by different agents who were motivated by different interests, some truly public spirited but, in the case of publishers, underpinned by commercial caution. In the first decade after the death one can see a contest between Ferdinand – as the unappointed but entirely altruistic guardian of the precious store of manuscripts, the nature of which, if not all the details, was known only to him – and the rest of the largely uncaring world.

Looking back over the century that had now elapsed we can see that, after Schubert's death, many of the enthusiastic friends and supporters who had enjoyed the Schubertiads had drifted away, many to well-paid positions and often no longer in Vienna. The friends had often retained copies of the *lieder* and some had become serious collectors of the manuscripts. But none can be seen to have taken any serious steps to promote the reputation of the dead composer or even offer constructive help to Ferdinand. He also had the immediate task of paying the medical bills that accumulated in Franz's final few days which, as we have seen, were barely covered by the prices he agreed with Haslinger and Diabelli. What is uncertain is whether even Ferdinand had any confidence that his brother's true stature would ever be revealed to the world, and indeed to what extent Ferdinand himself appreciated the real measure of his brother's genius.

A PATH STREWN WITH ROCKS

So, for the first six years after his death in 1828, there was little to show beyond occasional performances, including Liszt's transcriptions of the *lieder*; and a steady stream of publications, also largely of *lieder*. It was in 1835 that Ferdinand, still the sole guardian of the treasures, tried to drum up interest in performing the works in his possession by a series of advertisements, none of which produced any further response. It was not until Schumann's crucial visit to Ferdinand in 1839, just over 10 years after the death, that the situation began to change, and did so rapidly. It is not clear what Schumann had in mind, and indeed whether the visit was motivated by anything other than his admiration, as a young man, of the dances and piano works he had managed to procure. What we now know, is that Schumann's examination of the manuscript of the *Great* C Major Symphony lit a flame that would burn ever brighter as this unplanned discovery led to its performance, and to the gradual revelation of Schubert's genius.

For the rest of the story there were, by the 1840s, sufficient numbers of individuals who had acquired a knowledge of, and admiration for, Schubert's music – some in positions of influence – so it was becoming likely that public interest in the composer would return and begin to build. But the path would not be smooth and it would be many more years before public interest led to a general recognition of the composer's genius. During this time several individuals began the process of enquiring into the details of Schubert's life, but none were to succeed at this stage. The event that led to a major change of public perception of the composer was without doubt the publication of the first biography in 1865. It resulted in a wave of interest, both public and professional, and secured the backing of a sufficient number of influential supporters to launch the major project of collecting and then publishing the entire works. It was that project which occupied the next three decades and led to the astonishing discovery of the full extent of the compositions left to us by the composer.

THE PUBLIC'S PERCEPTION OF A NEW GENIUS

The discovery of the hitherto dimly appreciated national hero (in Austria), and the man who wrote such beguiling music (elsewhere), certainly caught the public's attention, especially coupled with tales of the Bohemian life he was reputed to have led. Many popular depictions of Schubert appeared, often in the guise of a handsome young dandy.

A popular depiction of Schubert

As always, the public was less concerned with the facts and relished the image of a well-dressed young genius sitting at his piano, regardless of the small detail that he had never possessed one of his own.

The image is consistent with that of Schwammerl in the operetta *Lilac Time* (see Chapter 16), in which Schubert became the eternally good-humoured character who helps others to achieve their dreams while foregoing his own. The image was also taken up by commercial interests around the turn of the twentieth century so that Schubert began to appear, smartly attired, on cigarette cards and became a familiar figure advertising the appeal of a range of suitable and unsuitable products, including the Austrian equivalent of OXO.

WHAT DID THE CENTENARY SIGNIFY?

Had Schubert, therefore, been discovered by the time of his centenary? The answer is certainly no. For there had, as yet, been no serious study of the man himself. All the biographical accounts so far had perpetuated the notion that Schubert was, as described by von Hellborn, poorly educated and had written down his compositions at great speed with no corrections, continuing the myth that he was in some way in receipt of divine inspiration. Only serious study of the manuscripts would dispel this nonsense. But in addition, while virtually all of the manuscripts had been published, there were great and significant gaps in the appreciation of the music. One obvious example is the last three piano sonatas, which had been strangely overlooked and misunderstood since their publication in 1838. Another gap was virtually the whole body of operas, an omission still awaiting remedy. Perhaps an interim conclusion would be that there was so much of Schubert now laid before the world that no-one then (or now) had managed to take it all in. That challenge still awaits a solution.

Thus we have seen Schubert's reputation grow from near obscurity and a serious danger of being forgotten in the years immediately after his death, through several stages of rediscovery, each promising a new dawn but with periods of inactivity and misplaced optimism. But his music always provided a bright path through any difficulties and led eventually to the harnessing of great musical forces to collect, collate and publish the complete works. This was largely achieved by the time of the two centenaries; but from that point the real work of understanding and appreciating Franz Schubert can be said to have begun in earnest.

CHAPTER 13
THE TWENTIETH CENTURY AND TODAY

Schubert scholarship during the nineteenth century was taken up with discovering who he was and what events happened during his short life; and in parallel, with unearthing, listing and collating the music he left to posterity at his death. These objectives had largely been fulfilled by the close of the nineteenth century so that the task of bringing all this knowledge together into a proper understanding of the measure and stature of this almost overlooked genius could then proceed. The material available by the end of the century would allow anyone prepared to travel and visit libraries, as well as finding performances of the music, to gain a reasonable appreciation of the composer and his work. We have seen how Schubert's music was taken up elsewhere in Europe, particularly in England, through a number of influential and enthusiastic supporters. But his memory was certainly not allowed to fade in Vienna.

We have seen how, in the 1870s and 1880s, Schubert became venerated as a national hero of Austria, with the erection of the Denkmal in the Stadtpark and the reburial of his remains (along with those of Beethoven) in the Zentralfriedhof. The veneration continued with the centenary celebrations in 1897 and in 1928. By this date the Austrians had invented a celebration of Schubert's life, the Sängerbundesfest, which took place every four years.

Schubert himself in procession in Vienna circa 1928

This was a festival in which male-voice choirs competed, singing Schubert's many compositions for male voices and enjoying a parade in which the composer figured prominently. The picture above shows the event in 1928, the second of the two centenaries. But to get a picture of the developing knowledge and appreciation of Franz Schubert in the twentieth century we need to take a wider view.

THE SCHOLARSHIP OF OTTO ERICH DEUTSCH

The documentary material which had emerged during the nineteenth century was still dispersed through an increasing number of books on the composer. But all that would change with the advent of the new century, through the endeavours of a scholar who is still regarded as having made the greatest contribution to the study of Schubert's life and works. Dr Otto Erich Deutsch was, in the first decade of the twentieth century, still in his twenties and an art critic for a Vienna daily newspaper as well as holding a minor academic post in the university. Whilst tempted to add to the literature on Schubert, whose music he revered, he observed that the available documents on Schubert and his life were not only dispersed but woefully incomplete. He therefore set out on a personal crusade to track down all the original documents that could then be traced as contributing to Schubert's life, starting with the many collections amassed by earlier intended biographers. He then proceeded with his own searches, as well as personally exploring all or most of the places visited by Schubert during his lifetime. This was accompanied by a plan to publish his discoveries in a series of volumes to be written over a number of years. The principal volume of documents, containing many previously unseen, was published, in German, by Georg Müller in Munich in 1914. But the grand plan was then interrupted by the First World War. Then, while able to continue in the 1920s and 1930s, the plan was even more seriously disrupted by enforced abandonment of Vienna and relocation, eventually in Cambridge, to escape the Nazi takeover of his native country and city.

As recorded elsewhere, the grand project was finally completed in the 1950s with the volume of Schubert documents being greatly enlarged and republished, first in English before being translated back in to German. The grand project also included the celebrated thematic catalogue which, for the first time, listed the (almost) complete works in order with their allotted Deutsch numbers; and as a new volume, the collected memoirs of Schubert's friends. Thus from 1914 and progressively onward into the 1950s, the complete documentation concerning Schubert's life was readily available in both German and English. The detailed knowledge of Schubert's life had thus been revealed during the first half of the twentieth century, to a degree which had not been appreciated during the whole of the nineteenth century.

MUSIC-MAKING AND THE ADVENT OF THE GRAMOPHONE

Returning to the early part of the twentieth century, while more performances of Schubert's music were taking place, before the advent of electronic reproduction, a musical performance was a unique event for which the listener had to be present. However, it is clear that Schubert's music had also reached audiences through the medium of home music-making. The piano was a standard item of furniture throughout Europe and making music at the piano, as well as performing on other instruments and certainly singing, was widespread and very much the fashion throughout most of the nineteenth century.

The huge volume of 'chamber' compositions written for piano, voice and other small combinations of performers, made Schubert's music particularly suitable for private amateur performance, and there can be no doubt that this was the medium through which his music was kept alive and fresh in between the occasional formal concert performance. But all that was to change with the invention of recording, to the extent that great music is today available on demand. The change, however, occurred at a measured pace and it was not for another half century that the revolution in listening to music came into its own.

The gramophone began to play its part in the popular dissemination of the music of Franz Schubert from the 1890s. Some of the earliest recorded performances are preserved and still available as vinyl discs. A collection issued by EMI Records Ltd in 1982* contains some 126 solo performances of songs, accompanied mostly by piano alone, but in a few cases by instrumental arrangements. The performances are given by many celebrated names, including Lilli Lehmann and Harry Plunket Greene, recorded well before the First World War in a variety of

---

* Schubert Lieder on Record, 1998-1952.

venues from London and Berlin to Dresden and Vienna. Both records and gramophones were relatively expensive and there would have been little immediate impact on the spread of musical appreciation, especially with the impact of the war. However, from the 1920s, the gramophone was joined by radio which could bring great music direct into the home, including live and recorded performances. The latter now included, during the 1930s, recorded performances of Schubert *lieder* by the current stars such as Elisabeth Schumann and, as a young accompanist, Gerald Moore who, after the Second World War, was to be joined by Elisabeth Schwarzkopf and Dietrich Fischer-Dieskau in now classic performances.

So, by the middle of the twentieth century, great music was available to all through an increasing number of media. The commercial recording companies could engage the current stars of the concert hall to record their own performances of all the great works. Increasingly the catalogues offered alternative performances to the discerning record-collector; and there was a corresponding expansion of the recorded works available, so that more and more of Schubert's full catalogue of *lieder* could be found on record. All this growth of recorded music has been accompanied by a corresponding growth in the popularity and the appreciation of great music. Thus in the case of Schubert, what might, at the start of the century, have been regarded as relatively obscure works (such as the String Quintet or the late piano sonatas) have become not just popular but have acquired iconic status.

Fortunately, while many are content to hear recorded performances, audiences have also been driven back in increasing numbers to live performances such that a recital of any of the Schubert song cycles can be guaranteed a healthy, if not capacity, audience. That such an outcome has been the result of the introduction of the gramophone, and of other media, is at one level remarkable; but at another level it is surely a reflection of the much wider appreciation of good music that electronic reproduction has brought about. All the media, from radio and television to many other forms of dissemination and collecting, have contributed to the present situation in which the works of Schubert and a host of other composers, great and not so great, have become familiar, with media channels devoted to nothing other than playing music that the general public will find attractive and entertaining.

A MYSTERY CARRIED OVER FROM THE NINETEENTH CENTURY

A seemingly vital question, raised in the 1880s, remained unsolved until well into the twentieth century: was there a missing Gastein Symphony? As we have seen, even O. E. Deutsch was, at the time of publishing his thematic catalogue, a firm believer in the lost symphony. Even by 1958 Maurice Brown, in his *Critical Biography of Schubert*, after reviewing the evidence, declared that it was not possible to come to a definite conclusion as to the existence of the alleged lost symphony.

The issue had first been raised in 1881 by George Grove when preparing the biographical article on Schubert for his dictionary. Perhaps there was an expectation, carried over from the 'discovery' of the *Unfinished* Symphony less than 20 years earlier, that there might be more gems still to be unearthed. Grove had read the references, in the biographical notes prepared by the poet Eduard von Bauernfeld and by Josef von Spaun, to a 'Grand Symphony,' written when the composer was in Gastein (on tour with Johann Michael Vogl) in 1825, for which the composer declared that he 'had a special liking.' Grove had examined the manuscript of the *Great* C Major Symphony in the library of the Vienna Musikverein and saw that it was dated March 1828. The recorded recollections of Schubert's colleagues from 1829 led Grove to the conclusion there was another work from 1825, now referred to as the Gastein Symphony which had, like the *Unfinished*, been lost and was awaiting discovery. Grove wrote a letter to *The Times*, dated 28 September 1881, referring to the apparent loss. This led to a misunderstanding as to whether the Musikverein was being accused of negligence, which was not the case; but in the result the issue became notorious and was the subject of much debate and not a little investigation.

Part of the original mystery arose from an undated letter from Schubert in which he dedicated the symphony to the Gesellschaft der Musikfreunde; but that body had no record of receiving it in 1826. What is clear is that Grove, on his visit to Vienna in 1867, had examined the copy of the symphony held by the Musikverein, on which Schubert had made his numerous changes and had then inscribed on the manuscript the date of March 1828. It is not recorded how the manuscript arrived at the Musikverein, but a fair copy of the symphony, with its alterations, had been made and retained by brother Ferdinand, which was the copy inspected by Schumann in 1839 and subsequently sent on to Mendelssohn. But this does not answer the question whether the symphony, before Schubert's changes, was written in 1825 or in 1828, and in the latter case, whether there was a missing work from 1825.

The mystery began to be resolved, as already discussed, by an analysis proposed by John Reed in his 1972 book *Schubert: The Final Years*, in which Schubert's output is analysed as falling into three periods, classically termed early, middle and late. Taking account of a number of works, including notably the B flat Piano Trio which he regarded as being written some time before the E flat Trio, Reed assigns both the B flat Trio and the *Great* C Major Symphony to the year 1825, that is, the middle period of Schubert's compositions, a view which has gradually been accepted. More recent research has reached the firm conclusion that the *Great* C Major Symphony is the work of 1825 or certainly of Schubert's middle period and therefore, taken with the other available evidence, that the *Great* C Major is one and the same as the Gastein Symphony. It is also to be concluded that the manuscript of the symphony was not presented to the Musikfreunde until March 1828, after Schubert had made the corrections which appear on the manuscript, and redated the work. This was the version performed by Mendelssohn in 1839 and which was given finally in Vienna by Hellmersberger in 1850, having already been published in Leipzig in 1840. It is interesting that even Dr Otto Erich Deutsch, in his seminal thematic catalogue of 1951, when assigning to the symphony D number 944, recorded that the work was 'Begun March 1828.' The correct assignment of the work to 1825 now confirms the recorded recollections of Messrs Bauernfeld and von Spaun as to the composition of a symphony in that year, and leads to the conclusion as to its identity.

It remains a mystery precisely when the manuscript was delivered to the Musikverein and when Ferdinand made the fair copy. Schubert himself wrote the date of March 1828 on the manuscript but the changes could have been made at any earlier date and the fair copy made after the changes. The likely sequence of events has already been discussed, including the probable date when the copy of the amended manuscript was made by Ferdinand. Whether or not more of the true story will ever emerge, the saga of the *Great* C Major and its manuscripts will remain a subject for research or at least speculation, and one which stands out against other areas of research for its human as well as its artistic interest. It is at least a relief to know that no symphony remains lost.

CONTEMPORARY SCHOLARSHIP

There is now no danger of Franz Schubert and his astonishing output of music being overlooked or passed over in any respect. Since the early twentieth century Schubert's music has become the subject of increasing academic scholarship, originally led by such giants as Otto Erich Deutsch and later by Maurice Brown and John Reed in England, and by scholars in other countries. Research is now well established in many university music departments throughout Europe and the USA. Particular research has been carried out into Schubert's handwriting (in Austria) which has thrown light on his personality, and periodic changes to it, as well as his musical style. In the USA, analysis carried out on samples of handmade manuscript paper used by the composer have yielded important new information about dating of works. For example, a collection of manuscripts held by the Vienna Musikverein dated 1819 was found, upon such analysis, to include the sketches of the Tenth Symphony which may have been the last work ever committed to paper before the composer's death in 1828.

In addition to physical research there have been regular symposia, often organised for anniversaries or special events and usually based in university departments. These include particularly the Cambridge celebration of the bi-centenary in 1997, memorialised in *The Cambridge Companion to Schubert*, a collection of papers by international academics, edited by Christopher H. Gibbs, and published along with a special edition of *The Musical Times*, organised by Leo Black for the event. The 200th anniversary of Schubert's birth was also marked by a large number of broadcast concerts promoted by the BBC, including performances of many completions of unfinished works.

THE CAMBRIDGE SYMPOSIUM

The published papers present a valuable record of contemporary scholarship and perceptions of Franz Schubert and his musical achievements up to 1997. Christopher Gibbs records in his introductory paper that Schubert's position, literally as well as symbolically, has changed dramatically since his death, and that over the course of the nineteenth century he gradually joined the elect, becoming an immortal composer, the peer of Beethoven and superior to his contemporaries Rossini and Paganini. Of the many nineteenth-century composers, Schubert is the one whose lifetime fame was significantly at odds with his later glory. The papers then presented for the symposium seek to explain how this came about and how it took most of the remainder of the century to establish Schubert's rightful place.

From the Vienna of Schubert's day, his legacy has been appropriated by different political and cultural groups in many different ways, but Schubert's universal genius has transcended all such attempts. Popular images and legends grew up and have persisted about Schubert's lack of ambition, modesty and lack of achievement. Whilst largely false, they have given rise to a corresponding failure to appreciate the true qualities of his music, a failure only corrected in the latter years of the twentieth century as the canon of Schubert's most admired compositions has changed. Schubert's circle of companions and his passion for friendship is a perennial topic of debate. How far did friendship go? Was its main purpose literary and did it influence Schubert's compositions? The originality of Schubert's classical forms is shown by analysis of compositions, from *lieder* to piano duets and including the E flat Trio to the final piano sonatas. As to the poetry selected for the *lieder*, it becomes evident that Schubert's tastes changed as his career progressed, adapting or recomposing some of the material and often returning to the same source. All these topics raise more issues which await further research.

In his *lieder* Schubert, from the outset, was able to transform the genre. However, a different 'social' genre is represented by the dances for piano, both solo and four-hand, and by the part songs for different combinations of voices. This popular genre contains many masterpieces and shows how Schubert composed for the audiences of his time. Of the piano sonatas, the uncompleted and fragmentary movements may be seen as occupying a place in his creative development. The solo and duet piano works reflect an almost unfailing consistency of accomplishment whilst departing from Beethoven's model. For the chamber music, in contrast to the great quartets, trios and other late works, some 12 quartets and an early quintet had been composed before the first group of successful *lieder* up to 1816. For the later works Schubert became acquainted, in 1824, with Ignaz Schuppanzigh, whose string quartet performed the late Beethoven works and would perform Schubert's own later quartets as well as the Octet.

Whilst in Schubert's lifetime his following was largely restricted to personal supporters, his final immortality was recognised only in the closing years of the nineteenth century. There were few reviews of the works during his lifetime; those from German critics being less superficial than the critics in Vienna. However both were limited to published works, which meant that *lieder* remained the medium through which he became known. After his death, however, the spread of the *lieder* in particular became enhanced with reworkings by Liszt, Berlioz, Brahms and countless others. The eventual recognition of Schubert's place in the musical pantheon was hastened in particular by German scholarship. In England, knowledge of Schubert's music was initially limited to *lieder* and piano compositions. However, from the 1850s Schubert's music was promoted by Charles Hallé and Augustus Manns, supported by George Grove, with performances of much of the orchestral music including all the symphonies. Schubert became phenomenally popular in the last decades of the nineteenth century. Interest was again revived in the 1920s and has so remained. Schubert's reception in France, by contrast to England, was initially through his chamber music with *lieder* becoming more popular after 1835 as more were published in the French language. The masses received little attention and of the orchestral works only the *Unfinished* Symphony had achieved popularity up to the centenary of 1928.

THE OXFORD PROJECT

In 2014 Oxford University was host to the Schubert Project which, over four weeks, presented a series of song recitals which included the whole of Schubert's *lieder* repertoire together with all the celebrated chamber repertoire and more. The festival also marked the launch of an academic project with the title *Drama in the Music of Franz Schubert* for which many leading academics contributed articles, which were collated and edited by Joe Davies and James William Sobaskie and published in 2019. The papers present a wide range of research into Schubertian themes with authors from seven countries and covering stage and sacred works, *lieder* and instrumental works.

The stage works include a 'lost' Singspiel, *Claudine von Villa Bella*, as well as *Fierrabras*; and the sacred works, the fifth Mass in A flat, representing a span from 1815 to final completion of the mass in 1825. The early *Claudine* is seen as illustrating Schubert's precocious understanding of musical theatre; and *Fierrabras* as an important step in the development of fusion between dramatic music and text.

The dramatic theme is taken up through the early *lied Adelwold und Emma* (D211) and the incomplete *Gretchen im Zwinger* (D564); and the dramatic theme is further developed through the *Ständchen* (D889) and *Schwanengesang* (D957); and *Tempesta* in the *lieder* in *Gruppe aus dem Tartarus* (D583). The works thus span the neglected to the familiar, but demonstrate Schubert's remarkable range from a confident launch into a new field to the ordered development of his dramatic strategy and his grasp of music's potential to express and to move the listener.

The C Minor Impromptu (D889) is seen as demonstrating the thematic transformations and modulations, which would play a crucial role across the nineteenth century. Among familiar works analysed are movements of the last piano sonatas (D958-960) and of the String Quintet (D956), all composed within the final few weeks of the composer's life and representing the very climax of his genius. A theme running through the collection is Schubert's use of the *fermata* or pause, of which it is said: 'it is as though the music was listening into itself for something other than what it is saying, something of which it is reminded and which it tries to recall.'*

MORE CONTEMPORARY SCHOLARSHIP

For an account of even more recent Schubert scholarship, a collection of presentations was given in November 2020 to members of the Schubert Institute UK. Ongoing research topics included: the role of performance in Schubert's compositions for the piano; an exploration of the piano duet repertoire, a body of works spanning the whole of Schubert's composing career, much of which remains largely unexplored; Schubert's Orientalist *lieder* including the *Suleika lieder* and *Geheimes* (D717-720) of 1821; analysis of setting of poems of Franz von Schober (D786 and 792) giving vent to political dissent in the guise of eroticism; setting of *Stabat Mater* (D175 and 383) as revealing the composer's religious convictions.

These contributions represent research from the universities of Liverpool, Maynooth, Eire, Oxford and Cambridge and present a wide spectrum of studies demonstrating the areas of the composer's life and compositions still largely unexplored and of continuing interest. While not rivalling the drama of a 'lost' symphony, it can be concluded that the range and variety of research being undertaken currently in universities in the UK and elsewhere shows an increased interest in the music, rather than the history and background, and will in its course lead to a greater understanding and appreciation of this endlessly fascinating composer.

---

* Xavier Hascher on the first movement of D959, *Drama in the Music of Franz Schubert*, p 259.

PERFORMANCES OF SCHUBERT'S MUSIC IN ENGLAND

Quite apart from scholarship, the question remains: how frequently were the works of Franz Schubert performed in various concert venues? A survey of all the leading concert venues of the world is beyond this short review. But we have already seen that after a faltering start the spread of Schubert's music in England took off under the leadership of two German émigré musicians (Charles Hallé and Augustus Manns) and of an inspired amateur polymath, George Grove. Concerts at the re-sited Crystal Palace from the mid 1850s onwards were well supported and, as we have seen, presented frequent performances of Schubert's orchestral music including premieres (after Schubert's lifetime) of most of the early symphonies. The question is, was that level of popularity sustained into the new century and beyond?

From the 1880s onwards, a helpful contemporary source of information on the growing popularity of Schubert's music is found in the records of (mostly) chamber concerts at the South Place Ethical Society in the City of London – subsequently relocated in Holborn and renamed Conway Hall – which gave free concerts every Sunday evening. Their records show nine performances of the String Quintet between 1887 and 1927, as well as similar numbers of virtually all the great chamber works. The society's records show regular concerts devoted to Schubert's works, including *lieder*, and a series of concerts including almost the whole chamber repertoire organised for the 1897 centenary celebrations. There can be no doubt that Schubert's chamber music was being admired and enjoyed regularly in London, and no doubt elsewhere in England.

Another valuable source of information is the archive of London's Promenade concerts (the Proms), then given mostly in Queen's Hall London from 1895 and taken over by the BBC after 1922, conducted by the celebrated Sir Henry Wood. The Proms, however, tell a somewhat different story about the orchestral music. At the start of the series Schubert figured prominently, with the *Unfinished* Symphony being performed three times in the first series, together with the *Great* C Major Symphony, an operatic overture and many individual *lieder* (performed with piano accompaniment). But after the first series in 1895 (which had barely featured Beethoven or Bach), Schubert seemed to drop out of fashion with no particular events recorded for either the 1897 or the 1928 centenary. A routine seems to have been established of performing the *Unfinished* Symphony and the *Great* C Major once in each season, with additional piano-accompanied *lieder* and an occasional surprise item such as the Liszt version of the *Wanderer* Fantasia.

In May of 1930, by contrast, a different series of Northern Proms began in Manchester Free Trade Hall, conducted by the celebrated Sir Hamilton Harty. These concerts adopted the earlier pattern of the London concerts, with regular performances and repeats of the *Unfinished* and *Great* C Major Symphonies and additional *lieder*, together with regular performances of the incidental music to *Rosamunde*, *Marches Militaires* and other favourites. What none of these concerts attempted was the exploration of the rest of the orchestral oeuvre, with the exception of Symphony No 4 in C Minor (the so-called *Tragic*). It was indeed only in the last two decades that the remainder of the early symphonies began to appear in Proms programmes.

Yet another contrast is found (not unexpectedly) in the records of London's Wigmore (up to 1916 Bechstein) Hall from 1901. In its first decade, a relatively constant diet of Schubert's works emerged with regular performances of the great quartets (A Minor, D Minor and G Major) and of the String Quintet, plus occasional appearances of the piano trios. These were performed by a variety of ensembles, some already famous (the Joachim Quartet) and others with celebrity members including Pablo Casals, Frank Bridge and Percy Grainger. Pianists included Busoni and Moiseiwitsch. The *lieder* and individual piano works appeared regularly with frequent performances of the well-known classics and a few surprises such as the repeated rendering of *Der Leiermann* from *Winterreise*. In addition to chamber works, audiences were given occasional orchestral concerts, which included Symphonies No 5 and No 1 as well as operatic overtures; but it was not until 1911 that a full evening of Schubert's works was given. The A Major Piano Sonata (then noted as Opus posth) was performed by Artur Schnabel in 1904 but it was not until 1913 that the B flat Sonata appeared, followed later by the C Minor.

With the outbreak of war in 1914 concerts continued, following the same pattern and including celebrity performers such as Myra Hess, but with some interruptions. After the 1918 armistice a performance of the *Unfinished* Symphony was given and, in 1920, the first London performance of the Octet, together with a widening of the piano repertoire to include sets of dances and duets. Later in the 1920s many pianists began to play the B flat Sonata and celebrities appearing included Dohnányi, Kempff, Elisabeth Schumann and the young Clifford Curzon. From 1927 the two song cycles, *Die schöne Müllerin* and *Winterreise*, were performed regularly; and for the centenary events of 1928 several full evenings of Schubert *lieder* were given with accompanists now including Gerald Moore. The years up to the Second World War saw regular performances of the B flat and the E flat Piano Trios as well as the *Trout* Quintet, together with regular selections of *lieder*.

Performances were able to continue during the war, with some interruptions, but from 1946 the present familiar pattern of Schubert's works became well established, with regular *lieder* recitals, some presenting Schubert's work alongside other composers but often Schubert alone, with the song cycles invariably presented alone. The major chamber works have been presented regularly as have the piano sonatas, now including the full list with all the sonatas being afforded equal exposure. And the repertoire is continually extended with 'new' works becoming popular, such as the Arpeggione Sonata, played on cello or viola, and many more of the *lieder* being performed.

CONCLUSION

The twentieth century, therefore, saw both a continuation of the pattern of performances established at the Crystal Palace in London and elsewhere, and important changes in the works being offered to public audiences. Those changes reflect the combined perceptions of the performing artists, the concert promoters and the public, and reveal without question that Franz Schubert is now regarded as one of the great composers of the last two centuries, whose stature is universally accepted. The advent of electronic media has further advanced his popularity, which continues to fill recital rooms and concert halls. Changes in the popularity of individual works of course continues, but there will always remain a huge volume of works still awaiting exposure to wider audiences, and many new pleasures to be experienced as the repertoire grows. The volume of academic interest in Schubert and his works also continues, now in many different centres, generating new fields of scholarship. Schubert remains alive both in concert halls and in academia.

PART IV THE WORKS

CHAPTER 14
THE PIANO WORKS

At this point in our story we turn to review the different ways in which particular types of composition have fared in their appeal to the public since the composer's death – dealing first with the piano works, followed by the *lieder,* the operas and masses and finally the symphonies. Each of these genres tells a different story in terms of the reappearance of the compositions and the gradual appreciation of their true stature – in the case of the operas, one that is still at an early stage of evolution. But collectively they reveal the piecemeal way in which the genius of Schubert has been revealed to the world over decades and now centuries.

While Schubert played the violin and the viola and sang throughout his short life, the instrument with which he was most at home was the piano, which appeared in the majority of his compositions, whether they were for piano alone or accompanying other instruments or voices. It seems certain that Schubert never possessed a piano of his own, despite stories that his father had presented him with an instrument after the performance of his first mass in 1814. The truth is that all the great works for the instrument were composed and played by the composer on a borrowed piano. The story of the Rieder piano is set out in Deutsch's *Memoirs by his Friends** as an anonymous contribution, originally published in the press in 1897. The successful painter W. A. Rieder, who painted the famous watercolour portrait in 1825, offered Schubert the opportunity of playing his instrument – made by Anton Walter & Son of Vienna – by an arrangement which involved drawing back the curtains of a certain room if the coast was clear. Schubert was then free to enter his apartment to use the instrument. Drawing the curtains over meant that the Rieder household was engaged and Schubert would have to wait. The piano was subsequently acquired by the City of Vienna Museum.

THE REPERTOIRE

Even before reviewing the solo piano works it must be borne in mind that throughout his life Schubert composed great numbers of *lieder* exclusively with piano accompaniments, many of which include fine and complex piano parts. They were composed throughout his life and there is no doubt that the piano was his first and in many ways his principal medium for musical composition. And when one turns to the solo piano works, many have been interpreted as embodying symphonic ideas and grander musical concepts than can be conveyed by the keyboard alone. This aspect of the piano works has led to a number of compositions being orchestrated. While this topic is capable of much development, the works which Schubert left us were expressed in the terms of solo or duet piano compositions and they are here so discussed.

There are some 23 piano sonatas, of which 13 were completed, with those unfinished comprising one or more complete movements and a number of seemingly brutally truncated (that is, abandoned) part movements. The solo sonatas are appropriately regarded today (although not always so) as the

---

* 1958 ed, at p 221.

core piano works and have been the subject of much research and scholarship, initially in reassembling unpublished works in which manuscript pages and even whole movements had become misplaced over the years following their composition.

At Schubert's death only three of the sonatas had been published, those assigned the opus numbers 42, 53 and 78, otherwise D845, 850 and 894, and respectively the Sonatas in A Minor, D Major and the Sonata in G Major called by the publisher *Fantasia*. The three last sonatas (D958-960), together with a Sonata in A Minor (D784), were published in 1839 and a further six up to 1861, the last being the unfinished *Reliquie* Sonata in C, leaving 10 unpublished and incomplete works. These works were then published in stages as part of the *Gesamtausgabe* in the 1890s, with other emerging fragments appearing in later years. Such is the current interest in the sonatas, whether or not complete, that this whole genre has been the subject of much study, including determining its proper sequence.*

Apart from sonatas, there are a substantial number of other solo piano compositions ranging from sets of Variations, Fantasias, individual movements (Andante, Scherzo) and including the well-known Impromptus, Moments Musicaux and the *Klavierstücke*, many of these being among the most popular and well-known of his compositions. Within the Fantasias (properly so-called) may be noted the famous *Wanderer* Fantasia in four connected movements, which was orchestrated in the 1850s as a concerto by Liszt. Apart from its superb and exhilarating musical qualities this work is to be credited with having pioneered the linking of movements into a continuous musical whole, an innovation followed up in later works of Schubert and subsequently by many later composers. To this formidable catalogue of compositions must be added some 60 sets of dances for piano, some of these containing 20 or more individual pieces;

---

* See Maurice Brown, *Essays on Schubert:* 'Towards an edition of the Pianoforte Sonatas.'

and some 40 separate four-hand compositions, including the celebrated *Lebensstürme* (D947), the four-movement Grand Duo in C (D812) and the F Minor Fantasia of 1828 (D940), a work also in four connected movements.

Of these 'other' piano works, a distinctly higher proportion achieved publication during the composer's lifetime, compared to the piano sonatas. This includes some 11 sets of dances (which thereby came to the attention of the young Schumann), the *Wanderer* Fantasia and the first set of Impromptus, Opus 90. The much-loved four-hand Fantasia in F Minor was published shortly after the composer's death, with the four-hand *Lebensstürme*, the Opus 142 Impromptus and the three last sonatas following in a burst of publication of piano works in 1839.

The significance of these events is that a decade after the composer's death, the publishers, principally Diabelli, concluded, rightly, that there was a continuing market for Schubert's piano works, both solo and duet, and it is clear that the market was now an international one, extending at least to Germany and France and later to Britain.

As for the sequence in which these diverse piano works were taken up and performed, the order of publication gives the best clue, bearing in mind that publications began only in 1821 with *lieder* that had been composed and performed many years earlier. After the first rush of published *lieder*, 1821 also saw publication of the first of the many sets of dances for solo piano, followed by Piano Duets (including the famous Variations dedicated to Beethoven, D624) and the first major solo piano composition to be published, the *Wanderer* Fantasia (D760). The pattern of *lieder*, dances and duets was then repeated through the following years, but including the three piano sonatas published in 1825, 1826 and 1827. These were followed by the first set of Impromptus (D899) and the Moments Musicaux (D780), the second set of Impromptus (D935) being published posthumously together with a backlog of piano compositions that were to continue in publication for many decades after Schubert's death.

Whilst this short list may give some picture of the contemporary popularity of the piano compositions, we must bear in mind that what are today regarded as the greatest of the works, the three final sonatas D958, 959 and 960, were seemingly overlooked, even by Robert Schumann, a decade after the composer's death; and even after being published in 1839 were largely ignored. Only in the 1860s is it recorded that Charles Hallé performed 11 of the sonatas, which had by then been published in London, including the final three. But it was not until well into the twentieth century that the real greatness of these final sonatas began to be appreciated, and this must have encouraged both performers and audiences to explore more of the piano works.

CHAMBER WORKS

The piano was also an integral part of much of the chamber music repertoire, including the two great trios (D898 and 929) with the *Notturno* (D897), plus an astonishingly mature piano trio written in 1812 catalogued as D28; and works with piano accompaniment for flute (variations on *Trockne Blumen*), Arpeggione (or now cello) and violin. In the case of the violin, Schubert composed four relatively early sonatas, three of which were unjustly given the title *Sonatina* by the publisher, together with two major late compositions, the Fantasia in C (D934) and the *Rondeau brillant* (D895). Also to be included in this repertoire is the *Trout* Quintet, justly one of Schubert's most popular works. Of these further compositions, the *Rondeau brillant* was published in 1827, the *Trout* shortly after his death, as were the two piano trios, although the B flat Trio was inexplicably delayed until 1836, by which date the violin sonatas were also published. In terms of the progress in publications catching up with compositions, it may be noted that the String Quartets in A

Minor and D Minor were published in 1824 and 1831 with the G Major and the String Quintet having to await their debut performances in the early 1850s.

What emerges is that the publishers, allowing for proper commercial caution, were responding to a growing demand for works of Schubert other than *lieder* (for which sales throughout Europe were proceeding apace), although the demand and its satisfaction was being played out over a period of two decades and more. What is important for posterity is that the danger of Schubert being forgotten during the 1830s and 1840s, in the wake of new composers and new compositions, had surely passed and there was a growing appreciation and acceptance of the true qualities of this unique composer, even with the partial selection of his works that were then available.

UNDERSTANDING SCHUBERT'S DEVELOPMENT

As well as bringing Schubert's music before the public in a manner not achieved during the composer's lifetime, the discovery and analysis of the full extent of his piano compositions has enabled musicologists to analyse the development of Schubert's composing techniques. The piano compositions occupied Schubert from first to last: his first recorded composition, bearing the Deutsch number '1' is a piano Fantasia in G for four hands of 1810, and the final compositions the three great solo sonatas D958, 959 and 960 and the final song D965 with clarinet accompaniment.

The task of collating the piano compositions has included establishing the order of composition and thus assigning them to the different 'periods' of the composer's career, as earlier discussed. This analysis has led to the conclusion that a number of well-known works have been mis-dated, including the B flat Piano Trio which has been re-assigned to 1825 and therefore not contemporary with the E flat Trio of 1827. The revised dating of the piano works has revealed that in his middle and late periods the composer developed a new and original approach which, in the view of many, is seen as progressing beyond the world inhabited by his great predecessors into new and uncharted territory. An example of a new approach is the Andantino from the A Major Sonata D959. The work starts off conventionally with an ethereal hymn-like theme but suddenly plunges into an outburst of scales and staccato chords, before subsiding back to the opening mood. Alfred Brendel described the movement 'as spelling out the most acute emotional disturbance.' It remains an enigma which continues to challenge analysts.

THE LAST THREE SONATAS

There is general agreement today that the final sonatas, composed in the closing months of Schubert's life, epitomise not just the composer's final maturity but point towards the future of piano composition. However this was not to be their fate, for while some of Schubert's piano compositions spread throughout Europe in the middle years of the nineteenth century and undoubtedly influenced later composers, these three, perhaps his greatest achievements, remained in obscurity for the rest of the nineteenth century and even beyond.

Schubert referred to these sonatas, and the recently completed String Quintet, in a letter dated 2 October 1828 to the publisher Probst. The expressed purpose of the letter is to enquire about the appearance of the E flat Trio, which was to be Opus 100, but mentions almost as an aside that *'I have composed, among other things, 3 sonatas for pianoforte ... . If perchance any of these compositions would suit you, let me know.'* The letter also states: *'The sonatas I have played with much success in several places'* which, if true, would certainly have been private performances. They were not taken up by Probst but within a month of his death brother Ferdinand, on 17 December 1828, recorded a deal struck with the publisher Tobias Haslinger for the sale of 13 songs of what was to become *Schwanengesang*, together with the 'last three grand sonatas for the pianoforte' for an agreed fee of 500 florins, receipt of which was subsequently acknowledged. However, it appears Haslinger handed over the sonatas, not to Probst, but to Diabelli who published them with a dedication to Robert Schumann, the original dedicatee, Hummel, then being dead. Deutsch records that the sonatas were engraved by 1831 but not released until 1838.

After 1838, the three sonatas, which in the twentieth century were to take on a symbolic aura on a par with Mozart's last three symphonies, appear to have descended into obscurity. They were not even accorded the dignity of being assigned opus numbers, in contrast to a number of hitherto unpublished early piano works. The sonatas were strangely denigrated by Schumann, as already noted, and mostly ignored throughout most of the nineteenth century with the notable exception of Brahms, whom Clara Schumann remembered playing the B flat Sonata. Brahms became heavily involved in the *Gesamtausgabe* project which included editing the now-popular *Drei Klavierstücke* (D946); but any support he was able to offer to the final sonatas was to no effect.

THE FATE OF THE SONATAS

Von Hellborn, in his biography, drew attention to the works in the catalogue of pianoforte music where they are identified as 'Three Grand Sonatas,' but he gives the keys as C Minor, A Major and B Major, 'probably composed in the year 1828.' It seems he did not know the works. In Newman Flower's book *Franz Schubert: the Man and His Circle*, published in 1928 to coincide with the centenary of the composer's death, the author gives a detailed account of the life and compositions of his final year, 1828, but with the final piano sonatas and the String Quintet being mentioned only as a quote from Schubert's letter to Probst. And so it remained, even in the revised edition of 1949. By contrast, the modern view of these works is that they represented, in the words of Benjamin Britten, 'the most miraculous year in the history of music.' Their place in the repertoire is now unassailable.

Schumann's opinion would, in time, be severely revised by cooler-headed judges but it is likely that his initial expression was persuasive if not instrumental in the works being sidelined for the rest of the century, and for some time after that. While the sonatas were performed, by Augustus Manns as well as Brahms, there was no report of any public following or demand for them. They simply remained in the long list of compositions published in the *Gesamtausgabe* by 1894, to await their fate with many other compositions that had not yet caught the attention of performers or the public. Schumann's opinion has been roundly rejected by twentieth-century listeners and performers alike. Alfred Brendel, for one, expressed the hope 'that Schumann in his later years became better acquainted with the works and regretted his verdict.'*

The other works of the late period did not suffer delayed acceptance, although there was a pause of over 20 years in performing the G Major Quartet and the String Quintet. Once heard they became a regular part of the repertoire, now in countries beyond Austria. It remains strange that the Andante of the B flat Sonata (D960) did not appeal to audiences who clearly appreciated the original beauty of the Adagio from the String Quintet, when the two works were so obviously cast from the same mould. The explanation is that the Andante was simply not heard until well into the twentieth century.

THE TWENTIETH CENTURY

In the case of the final sonatas, the change of fortune was certainly assisted by recordings. The *lieder* had been recorded in Berlin, London and other recording venues by all the great

---

* *Alfred Brendel On Music* p 158.

singers of the day, from the 1890s onwards. No doubt they fitted conveniently onto the relatively short duration of the recordings available at that time. Recordings of chamber works soon followed but the piano sonatas were not recorded until the 1920s; the German pianist and composer Eduard Erdmann being credited with the first recording of the late sonatas, which he performed together with the G Major Sonata, D894. We have seen that the sonatas were, in fact, played at concerts in London's Wigmore (then Bechstein) Hall but their regular appearance did not occur until the 1920s, perhaps as a result of the recording.

Erdmann was followed by the Austrian American pianist Artur Schnabel, whose recordings of the last sonatas made in 1937 and 1939 are still regarded as classics. Schnabel is credited with the description of Schubert as 'the composer nearest to God.' Despite interruptions of the Second World War, the sonatas were now growing in popularity with audiences and soloists to the point where there were many different versions available on record, with more arriving each year. From the 1960s onwards the works were being played regularly in recitals and broadcasts. While some soloists perform the works separately as part of a recital (András Schiff, Alfred Brendel), other performers play the three sonatas in order in the same concert (Paul Lewis, Imogen Cooper). However performed, there is no question that the last sonatas have now become an important part of the repertoire and seem to generate almost a cult following among Schubert lovers.

The piano was thus the instrument through which Schubert chose, for practical reasons, to express the greater part of his musical output and through which his development as a composer can readily be traced. So it was that in the final months of his life he was to convey some of his most profound ideas in the form of the final three piano sonatas. While the reason for their obscurity throughout the nineteenth century remains a mystery, their revival conveniently coincided with the advent of recording so that from the 1930s they were launched into a new level of celebrity from which they continue to benefit as some of the most frequently heard pieces in the repertoire.

CHAPTER 15
THE LIEDER

Like the piano works, the *lieder* were composed throughout Schubert's life, and are among his very earliest compositions and seemingly the last as well. The numbers of *lieder* left to us is so extensive, and indeed astonishing, that no more than a brief account of the works themselves can be given here. In terms of Schubert's gradual emergence from the obscurity of Vienna in the 1830s, the *lieder* are the exception. However, the danger from that point onwards was that Schubert would be remembered and celebrated as a composer of *lieder* only, and that other fields in which he gave us such treasured compositions would be ignored and forgotten. Nevertheless the *lieder* do tell us much of the composer's life and development.

It seems clear that the *lieder* were always intended to be performed virtually as they were composed, and were indeed so performed by a variety of singers from Schubert himself and stalwarts such as Johann Michael Vogl, to more commercial performers in the case of many of the compositions that caught the public's attention. Many of the *lieder* date from his school days and here one of the pupils at the seminary, in a biographical note prepared for Ferdinand Luib, confirms that Schubert would try over his new songs with fellow pupils. The writer was not one of Schubert's intimates but was nevertheless 'electrified by the infinite charm' of the works, to the extent that he wrote them out himself for the benefit of his musical brother. The writer then identifies *Forelle*, *Erlkönig*, *Gretchen am Spinnrade*, *Jägers Abendlied*, *Wiegenlied*, *Alpenjäger*, *Tod und das Mädchen*, *Tod und der Jüngling*, *Adelaide* (not the one by Beethoven), the ballad *Der Liedler* and many others* as the songs so performed and transcribed.

The exception to *lieder* being performed as they were written, was the song cycles, which were not intended to be performed as individual numbers but as a narrative and, like a sonata or a symphony, as a complete composition, which would require more of a concert setting. Furthermore, by the time of composition of the first cycle, *Die schöne Müllerin*, a market for publication (and payment) had opened up, so that performances of the cycles, other than by Schubert himself for his friends, had to await the work being published. The final group of songs, given the title *Schwanengesang* by the publisher and often erroneously called the third cycle, whether or not that was Schubert's intention, was eagerly marketed and has remained a pinnacle of the art form. These songs do not form a narrative, nor is it apparent whether Schubert intended them to be performed together. But by the time of their composition song cycles were in demand and this resulted in their rapid publication. Though by then Schubert was dead.

DEVELOPMENT IN *LIEDER* COMPOSITION

Schubert composed *lieder* throughout his career, with gaps which were usually explained by his being preoccupied with writing operas. One significant conclusion that can be drawn from the

---

* The writer is Johann Leopold Ebner whose manuscript eventually formed an important source for the collected works: See Deutsch, *Schubert: Memoirs by his Friends*, p 46.

early *lieder* is that there is little evidence of the transition from apprentice to master. True it is that the first real and unquestioned masterpiece, the song *Gretchen am Spinnrade*, ranks in order of compositions as D118 and was recorded as being composed on 19 October 1814. This was the third year proper of his composing career and in terms of output, depending on how the *lieder* are to be counted, *Gretchen* ranked as No 44 of the songs. It was also composed shortly after his first Mass in F (D105). But its artistic maturity belies any idea of 'learning' how to compose such a piece, which in addition to its artistic merit was simply without precedent. The young Schubert had the innate ability to synthesise in his mind the qualities of a great song in which the voice and piano are perfectly matched, and to convey this onto the page with seemingly little preparation other than his own thought processes. While it might well have seemed to an observer of the process of composition that he was in receipt of divine guidance, we can conclude that his genius allowed him to short-circuit the process of working up sketches and ideas, and to see the final form of the song as he wrote the piece out.

Of course he did go through a process of learning his trade, which was itself extraordinary in terms of what emerged. His first two recorded songs, of 1810, are very lengthy settings of poems he had encountered, followed by an even lengthier one in 1811, all by poets who figured only infrequently thereafter. But early in 1811 he discovered the works of Friedrich von Schiller and Friedrich von Matthisson, both of whom were to figure regularly in later compositions. And after writing some 25 songs between 1812 and 1813, he began to compose at an accelerating rate of over 30 songs in 1814, the year in which he discovered Johann Wolfgang von Goethe. Schubert was to set some 70 of Goethe's poems, starting with *Gretchen am Spinnrade* and continuing throughout his career up to 1826. In each of the two 'miraculous' years of 1815 and 1816 he composed well over 100 songs, to say nothing of a host of other compositions including symphonies and masses. Songs from 1815 included the well-known and popular *Heidenröslein* (D257) and *Erlkönig* (D328) which alone received a rapturous reception, having truly caught the imagination of the public. The songs of 1816 included *An den Mond* (D296) and *Gesang der Geister über den Wassern* (D484), all to poems by Goethe, and *Der Wanderer* (D489) to a poem by Schmidt von Lübeck.

Schubert was to compose many pieces based on *Der Wanderer* – a further four songs bearing the title *Der Wanderer* and *Der Wanderer an den Mond* (D649 and D870), two entitled *Aus Heliopolis I* and *II* (D753 and 754) and the famous *Wanderer* Fantasia for solo piano (D760). A few other poems received the same devoted attention, appearing in successive song versions and sometimes as arrangements for various instrumental combinations. Celebrated examples are the introduction and variations on *Trockne Blumen*, originally part of *Die schöne Müllerin* but arranged for flute and piano as D802 and subsequently rearranged for violin and piano. Another perhaps even better known recycling of a song tune is *Der Tod und das Mädchen* (D531) of 1817, which was to reignite the composer's enthusiasm for such a seemingly droll tune in the form of the second movement of the *Death and the Maiden* Quartet (D810). This was some years later in 1825, when the composer was himself having to face the prospect of an early death. At one level it is possible to trace the development and expansion of Schubert's composing techniques through his reuse of familiar material; but at another level it shows how Schubert recognised and exploited what he saw as a good tune in which he perceived more possibilities than had been developed in the original composition.

ENDLESS VARIETY

It would be a mistake to think that Schubert served up all his songs in neat sizes that could be conveniently packaged for typical performances of 12 or 15 for an agreeable evening recital.

The 'songs' of 1815 included a setting of *Adelwold und Emma* (D211), a poem of Friedrich Anton Bertrand which has the dual distinction of being the longest of all the *lieder*, virtually a mini-opera of around 28 minutes, and the most neglected, by performers and academics alike. It has been referred to as a remarkable experiment in quasi-theatrical *lied*.* Between 1815 and 1817 Schubert composed eight such extended ballads, in addition to his compositions which were formally labelled as operas. The majority of the songs were, however, of a modest length ranging between one or two and 10 or more minutes. But to sit and listen to a group of songs from a particular period (now easily possible) fills one with an overwhelming sense of the variety of settings with successive 'D' numbers, that were composed around the same time. Schubert gives the impression of a mind overflowing with diverse ideas. The grand total of more than 600 *lieder* includes many surprises and compositions that hardly fit the modest description of song.

A male-voice part song performed in front of Schubert's final resting place at the Zentralfriedhof

---

* Susan Wollenberg, *Drama in the Music of Franz Schubert*, p 105.

In addition to the 600 songs (plus a treasury of other compositions), Schubert composed, throughout his career, a host of other choral pieces for a variety of performers, ranging from works for mixed voices (usually soprano-alto-tenor-bass), for male voices and for female or unspecified voices, totalling well over 200 compositions.

Among the ensemble numbers not ranking as *lieder*, might be mentioned the delightful *Ständchen* ('Zögernd leise' D920), composed in two versions when Schubert apparently mistook the request of his friend and lifelong supporter Anna Fröhlich for a setting for female voices only. It would be wrong to think that all the songs were about death or similar weighty subjects. *Ständchen* is about a young girl asleep in her bed while the chorus (in the version with lusty male singers) tries not to wake her! And humour is not lacking, as in the song *An Herrn Josef von Spaun, Assessor in Linz* (D749) of 1822, a jokey song asking, 'And do you never write, are you lost to us for all time?' Schubert's dear and loyal friend Josef von Spaun, now a well-to-do government official, had been posted to Linz and after that to Lemberg (then part of the Austrian Empire, now Lviv, Ukraine), returning only in 1827. In a way this was to even up the score, as Schubert had earlier set (the only occasion) in 1817 a more serious poem by Spaun called *Der Jüngling und der Tod* (D545) where death more characteristically declares: 'In my arms you will find cool gentle rest.' It is a poem more appropriate to Schubert than to Spaun, who lived on to 1865 and was able to contribute so much to Schubert's memory, as we have seen.

A NEW POET

After 1816 the annual tally of songs could not continue at the same rate, simply because Schubert took up other areas of composition, including operas. In 1817 more than 50 songs were written, but the numbers dropped to between 10 and 20 in each of the years between 1818 to 1822. However, at the end of this pause, the composer encountered a new poet who, while often credited with a more modest talent, was to be immortalised by Schubert. The poet was Wilhelm Müller, a native of Dessau (on the Danube) who was in fact greatly admired by Heine. Müller led a relatively routine life as a librarian and occasional poet, interspersed with incidents of high drama. His birth and death meant that his life span was strangely close to that of Schubert himself; and although his travels included a visit to Vienna, there is no suggestion the two ever met.

As a student in Berlin in 1815–16, Müller's circle of friends included the poet Ludwig Rellstab, whose seven poems were to be set, close to the end of Schubert's life, as the first book of the group of songs which became known as *Schwanengesang*. Müller's travels in 1817 took him not to Greece as intended but to Italy, despite which he continued to collect Greek folk songs. On returning to Dessau, he was to come into conflict with the authorities for his work in translating Byron, whose compositions were banned as subversive by the Biedermeier. Some may wonder why Schubert did not set any of Byron's works, which were then circulating in Europe and used extensively by composers who followed. Müller's experience may provide the answer; and although Byron failed to make it to Schubert's list of poets, his theme of the wandering philosopher was so well ingrained in the German psyche that it certainly appeared in many of Schubert's *lieder* including, as noted above, the songs based on *Der Wanderer*. Müller, of course, has Schubert to thank for his continued celebrity, albeit exclusively through the settings of his 20 poems comprising the cycle *Die schöne Müllerin*, and the 24 poems of *Winterreise*. Schubert was engaged in correcting the proofs of the second part of *Winterreise* shortly before he died. His last song, *Der Hirt auf dem Felsen*, which included a clarinet as part of the accompaniment, was a fusion of two poems, one of which was by Müller.* The two were combined by Schubert

---

* The other was by Varnhagen von Ense.

himself. Müller died a year before Schubert and did not hear any of the settings through which his name continues to be celebrated.

It is not clear how Schubert came to move from composing single, although sometimes very extended, *lieder* and operas, to the idea of a song cycle. There was one precedent which would have been well known to Schubert: Beethoven's *An die ferne Geliebte*. But by the time he embarked on the first of the cycles, *Die schöne Müllerin* (D795) written in 1823, he was a seasoned and mature composer with no need of precedents – not that the 400 or so songs composed up to that point had followed or heeded any precedent. A possible explanation is that Schubert became moved by the poems as a narrative, rather than the innate quality of the verses. One can see this in the attraction of the first part of the *Winterreise* cycle, which had inspired Schubert to set the first 12 poems without even knowing of the existence of the second set. Whether or not this holds good for the final settings, it is clear that the publishers of *Schwanengesang* were similarly inspired.

The most obvious division in the different types of *lieder* is between strophic or repeated verse songs and 'through-composed' (*durchkomponiert*) songs containing themes and episodes with no fixed structure. The former, closer to folk songs, are the melodies that most readily stick in the mind. The latter could be likened to blank verse or operatic arias, although no rules or patterns can begin to encapsulate the rich variety of the *lieder*. Strophic settings create a pattern in the music which Schubert exploits by subtle changes which the mind emphasises, for example by a characteristic and often dramatic switch from major to minor key.

The use and combination of strophic and through-composed *lieder* is nowhere better illustrated than in the song cycles. Here the songs form a poetic progression and, in both the Müller cycles, tell a story, the progress of which is not just accomplished through the settings but are given form and shape by Schubert's choice of the type of setting, whether strophic or through-composed. The songs within the cycles, which are briefly narrated below, give some opportunity to see and to share in the inspiration that they generated in the composer and which led to the creation of these pinnacles of the German art song.

DIE SCHÖNE MÜLLERIN

The 20 poems of Müller's cycle set by Schubert tell the story in progressive scenes of a carefree boy wandering along a brook (*Das Wandern*) wondering where it will lead him (*Wohin*) when he encounters the mill (*Halt!*) where he is set to work, and gives thanks to the brook (*Danksagung an den Bach*). He has now fallen in love with the fair Müllerin (*Am Feierabend*) and asks the brook if she loves him (*Der Neugierige*). Becoming impatient (*Ungeduld*) he greets the Müllerin (*Morgengruss*) and presents her with flowers (*Des Müllers Blumen*) and tears (*Tränenregen*). He has won her (*Mein!*) but can sing no more (*Pause*). Will their love fade? (*Mit dem grünen Lautenbande*). His reverie is disturbed by the arrival of a hunter (*Der Jäger*) who threatens to win the girl (*Eifersucht und Stolz*). His happiness drains away as he muses on the beloved colour (*Die liebe Farbe*), the hated colour (*Die böse Farbe*) and the withered flowers (*Trockne Blumen*). He returns to the brook (*Der Müller und der Bach*), which sings a lullaby as he sinks beneath the water (*Des Baches Wiegenlied*) with the refrain 'Gute Nacht, Gute Nacht.' The cycle as written contains several more poems: Schubert selected those he needed for his work.

The songs are given alternating and contrasting settings starting with a strophic melody suggestive of tramping, in which we can hear hints of the mill wheels. As the drama unfolds we reach a false climax with repeated words 'Dein ist mein Herz.' The story then continues up to the entry of the hunter which leads to two contrasting songs: *Die liebe Farbe*, with a slow strophic setting in which one note is repeated in semiquavers throughout the whole song, to mesmerising effect; and *Die böse*

Farbe which is given a fast and dramatic setting. This is followed in a slow minor key by *Trockne Blumen*, which switches half way to the major key with a new melody at the words '*and when she walks past (his grave)*.' The cycle ends with *Der Müller und der Bach*, a dialogue between the miller in a minor key and the brook answering in the major against a haunting melody; and finally the brook sings a slow lullaby in strophic form as the work closes.

The cycle, which is now usually performed as a whole, created a new art form, extending the concept of a song cycle far beyond anything that had come before, including *An die ferne Geliebte*. It took a little time for the Viennese public to accept such a departure, but its early publication and follow up with a second cycle shows how the beauty of the music and the originality of the concept soon caught on, helped by the growing appreciation of the *lieder* beyond Vienna. Schubert's choice of *Trockne Blumen* as the basis of a major set of variations for violin and piano (D802), also tells us something of the composer's own appreciation of his creations, in the same way as his choice of other *lieder*, such as *Der Tod und das Mädchen* and *Der Wanderer*, as the theme for other extended works. The popularity of *Die schöne Müllerin* and the two following cycles is also shown by Franz Liszt's piano transcriptions which, from the 1830s, were performed by him and by other pianists throughout Europe and beyond.

While these two great Muller cycles and also the *Schwanengesang* collection were intended to be heard as a continuous recital, it is only since the second half of the twentieth century that it has become common to perform a full cycle. Individual numbers or groups of songs are still often presented. Where this is the case the cycles as narrated here will allow the individual songs to be seen in their intended context.

WINTERREISE

The 24 poems were set in two parts, simply because Schubert embarked on and completed setting the first 12 songs before discovering a second set of 12. They form a continuous narrative, however, and are musically a continuous dramatic work. The songs were originally published with a different ordering but are set out here in the order in which they are usually performed, and as Schubert intended.

The opening song, perhaps intentionally echoing the close of *Die schöne Müllerin*, is *Gute Nacht*, a strophic song of farewell as the traveller quits his home and his faithless beloved to embark on a winter journey, the final verse changing from minor simply to major, perhaps to express some last hope. The next nine songs are through-composed with dramatically varied settings. *Die Wetterfahne* is a reflection on the weathervane of the beloved's house, followed by tears in *Gefror'ne Tränen*. At *Erstarrung* the pace quickens with a duet between the base line and the singer, accompanied by fast triplets, relieved by a short passage in the major key. *Der Lindenbaum* brings rest beneath its branches, again disturbed by fast triplets. *Wasserflut* presents a slow and reflective tune in two sections, with a repeat. *Auf dem Flusse*, the river now icy and still, is set to a simple *pianissimo* figure which grows to a forte climax as he reflects on the turbulence beneath the surface, and in his heart. *Rückblick* has a dramatic setting in open syncopated chords creating a disturbed outcry which then passes from minor to major to end in peaceful reflection. *Irrlicht* depicts a will-o'-the-wisp which threatens to lead him astray in a slow almost stately setting. *Rast* is even slower as tiredness takes over and rest induces sleep. The sunny melody of *Frühlingstraum* is violently broken into by a crowing cockerel, followed by an ethereal *pianissimo* melody, which is repeated as dreams of the beloved return. But *Einsamkeit* is a slow reflection on his loneliness with a forte cry of wretchedness. So ends the first part of *Winterreise*.

While Deutsch allotted the same D911 to both parts of the work, there was a gap in the composition and they were published separately. Part 2 opens with *Die Post*, a lively prancing tune suggestive of horses which, sadly, bring him no letter. In *Der greise Kopf,* frost has given the impression of age in a slow reflective theme. In *Die Krähe* a crow accompanies the journey in a slow, circular tune. In *Letzte Hoffnung*, falling leaves suggest falling hopes in a skeletal syncopated accompaniment, with a sad conclusion. In *Im Dorfe* we arrive at a village, where barking dogs are reflected in the rumbling accompaniment which leads to a quiet ending. *Der stürmische Morgen* changes the mood with a fast springing theme which forebodes more bad weather. *Täuschung* has a dance-like tune which deludes the wanderer. *Der Wegweiser* gives us a short strophic song with verses in minor and major keys, which points finally to a road from which there will be no return.

The final bars of *Der Wegweiser* in Schubert's own manuscript with the words '*Eine Strasse muss ich gehen, die noch keine ging zurück*'

Das Wirtshaus is an inn which, to a hymn-like setting, becomes a graveyard where all the rooms are full. *Mut* is a defiant setting which battles against wind and storm. *Die Nebensonnen* presents a disturbing illusion, set to a solemn tune as he nears the journey's end. Finally, in *Der Leiermann*, he encounters the sparse drone of the hurdy-gurdy. He asks, 'Shall I go with you?'

Winterreise has, of all the *lieder*, become the subject of many alternative settings for new and original combinations of voices and instruments.* We have seen in particular that the final song, *Der Leiermann*, became a favourite programme filler in the early 1900s; but a century later the same song appears to have engaged the interest of a different generation of enthusiasts, including an arrangement for 4 bass saxophones and extending to the re-discovery of the hurdy-gurdy to accompany the songs.† The cycle has also inspired performers to convey their thoughts and reactions to the music in print.‡ Whether this is due to the music alone and the contribution of the poetry is a matter which invites various opinions.

SCHWANENGESANG

In the last months of his life Schubert turned again to the idea of a collection of songs, but not this time as a cycle with a narrative but as two collections, of seven poems by Rellstab and six by Heine, and one by Seidl. There is no common theme save that the songs are, in terms of emotional piquancy and drama, unsurpassed by any other of the *lieder*. The songs can be performed in different ordering but are usually presented as separate groups by the two poets. The usual sequence of the Rellstab poems is *Liebesbotschaft, Kriegers Ahnung, Frühlingssehnsucht* and the

---

* *Winterreise* by Le Chimera Project with Philip Sly and others.
† *Winterreise* performed by Matthias Loibner and Natasa Mirkovic.
‡ Ian Bostridge and others.

famous *Ständchen*, followed by *Aufenthalt, In der Ferne*, and *Abschied*. The Heine poems open with the dramatic *Der Atlas*, followed by the tormented *Ihr Bild*. The mood lightens with *Das Fischermädchen* which is followed by *Die Stadt, Am Meer* and the most dramatic of the whole sequence *Der Doppelgänger*. The set was completed by Haslinger, the publisher, adding the setting of Seidl's poem *Die Taubenpost*. The songs are united by the fact they are, with the exception of *Der Hirt auf dem Felsen*, the last to be composed and, as if to emphasise the loss to humanity, among the finest and most powerful of the composer's creations.

THE *LIEDER* COMPOSERS

Schubert was, for many, the composer who established German art song, soon followed by Schumann and then by many other great composers of the German world, who further developed the new art form up to and beyond the end of the nineteenth century. However, Schubert was not the creator of the German art song. At the start of his composing career there was an existing genre of German song stretching back to C. P. E. Bach, Mozart and, as already noted, Beethoven. But it was Schubert who transformed the genre into the major art form it has become. An account of Schubert's place in the German hierarchy of *lieder* composers is given in an essay by Dietrich Fischer-Dieskau which forms an introduction to *The Fischer-Dieskau Book of Lieder*, with English translations of over 750 of the songs. The essay also serves to counter the contention, sometimes heard, that Schubert's choice of text was uncritical and unliterary. Schubert was as literary as any of the great *lieder* composers. He also had the capacity to set some 150 songs to minor poems by friends; but also, according to his friends, rejected many requests for settings. It is clear that he selected only poems by which he was moved or inspired, as demonstrated by the many poems he set in multiple versions,* and by the narrative poems of Müller through which Schubert opened up the whole new world of the song cycle.

For the subsequent development of German *lieder*, mention should be made of Carl Loewe, who was a close contemporary of Schubert but who was to survive him by three decades. In many ways Loewe was everything that Schubert was not: reputedly handsome, supported by patrons and winning wide acclaim in north Germany. This was followed in the 1840s by foreign tours which included Vienna in 1844, where his reception provided a shameful contrast to the continuing neglect of Schubert's music. Nevertheless, Loewe together with Schumann and later Hugo Wolf, a serious admirer of Loewe, built on Schubert's creation of the new genre and ensured, once the true measure of Schubert's greatness was more apparent, the survival and flourishing of the German art song through later masters including Mendelssohn and Brahms and subsequently Mahler and Richard Strauss.

We have seen how Schubert's *lieder* caught the attention of the Viennese public and how they spread throughout the German-speaking world (aided by Liszt's piano transcriptions) and subsequently through France and, rather more slowly, through England, often only through particular favourites such as *Erlkönig*. From an early date the song cycles also attracted attention, although it was only from about 1856 that performances included the full cycle. As Schubert had predicted, *Winterreise* became popular, reflecting the growing romantic movement of the nineteenth century which Schubert had played a major part in launching, and which Byron had fired up to the point of engulfing the whole of Europe. So it was that *Winterreise* in particular began to acquire a cult status, which continues to grow today. It was supported by a host of artists and musicians, starting with Johann Michael Vogl, who continued to perform

---

* For example, there are 6 settings of Goethe's *Nur wer die Sehnsucht kennt*.

the cycle right up to his death, through Samuel Beckett who saw parallels with the bleak world in which his dramas were set, to Ian Bostridge who has added to his many performances throughout the world a volume dedicated to *Winterreise* entitled *The Anatomy of an Obsession*.

Lieder recitals during the second half of the nineteenth century enjoyed a steadily increasing range of music from which to select. Performances would usually draw on the works of several composers but it is clear that Schubert remained a favourite either through the choice of a few favourite *lieder* or one of the song cycles. This trend continued well into the gramophone era of the twentieth century, which also served to spread the appreciation of the lesser known of the *lieder*. This has led to an increased interest in, and study of, the whole *lieder* repertoire. From the end of the twentieth and into the twenty-first century, recitals have thus begun to explore the full range of the *lieder*, with complete recordings of the *lieder* and festivals at which the whole of Schubert's output has been performed. The *lieder* can today be said truly to be back with us, as a permanent tribute to his genius.

CHAPTER 16
THE MASSES AND THE OPERAS

These two major groups of compositions are dealt with together as they bear a significant relationship, each presenting a dramatic musical form which tells a story. The quantity of music contained in both the masses and the operas is very substantial and each genre occupied a significant proportion of the composer's time at different periods throughout his composing career. Surely Schubert himself would have expected their reception to be at least similar. Yet they could not be more different. Both required substantial forces for their production and an appropriate venue, either a theatre or a large church. Yet the masses, together with a large number of his smaller religious compositions were, in most cases, promptly performed and well received, mostly repeated and many performed in churches outside Vienna; whereas only a few of the operas were staged in Schubert's lifetime and those exclusively in Vienna. Those which were performed secured only a handful of performances. None were deemed successful in Schubert's lifetime and this has continued to be the general response of the public as the potential audience. There is a widespread and well-justified opinion that the masses represent some of Schubert's greatest works, particularly the final two masses in A flat and E flat respectively. But the operas are seen, in some quarters, as an unfortunate miscalculation by Schubert and a part of his output which is best overlooked. There is a converse view that there is simply no basis to regard the operas as other than equal in stature to the masses and other major works. But it is not the general view and therefore needs to be examined with some care.

THE MASSES

Six full masses were composed during the span of Schubert's composing life, together with two German masses or requiems. In between these major compositions Schubert composed more than 30 separate sacred works for church use (including *Salve Regina*, *Stabat Mater*, *Tantum Ergo* and *Benedictus*). Many of the masses and other sacred works were published in the composer's lifetime or shortly afterwards. The first to be performed was the celebrated Mass in F (D105), composed in 1814 for the centenary of the local Lichtental Church in which Schubert had been raised as a chorister and organist. The mass was first performed in October 1814 and within days of this event, Schubert composed the song *Gretchen am Spinnrade* (D118), which is regarded as his first masterpiece in the *lieder* repertoire.

Such was the enthusiastic reception of the first mass that he embarked on a second Mass in G (D167) in early 1815, which today is one of the most popular; and a third Mass in B flat (D324) at the end of the same year. The fourth Mass in C (D452) was composed in the summer of 1816. A 'Deutsches Requiem' in G Minor (D621) followed in 1818 after which Mass No 5 in A flat (D678) was completed, only after substantial revisions, in 1822. Another Deutsche Messe was composed in 1827 (D872) and finally the sixth Mass in E flat (D950), written in the miraculous final year of 1828.

The earlier masses all received prompt performances, beginning with the first mass of 1814, which was given a repeat performance at another local church in the same year, both under the direction of the 17-year-old composer. The Lichtental Church was the venue for the second mass, in early 1815, the third mass at the end of the same year and the fourth Mass in C, completed in the summer of 1816. The 'Deutsches Requiem' in G Minor of 1818 was similarly performed in September of that year. After a long pause the fifth mass was completed for its first performance at the Altlerchenfelder Pfarrkirche in 1823. The fourth mass received a second performance at the Maria Trost Kirche on 8 September 1825 together with other sacred works, the *Salve Regina Offertorium* (D223), *Tantum Ergo* in C (D739) and *Graduale* in C (D184).

The fifth Mass in A flat was an exception to the earlier masses in several ways. First it was composed initially in November 1819 but then laid aside and completed only in September 1822, which was itself a departure from the usual fate of uncompleted works. By this date Schubert had completed – so far as he ever would – the *Unfinished* Symphony and was about to launch the *Wanderer* Fantasia (D760). His compositions had taken on a new maturity, reflected in John Reed's analysis which designated this as Schubert's middle period. Schubert himself considered that the A flat Mass had turned out well and considered a dedication to the Emperor. However, this was not pursued and he was unable to supervise the first performance in 1823, owing to the onset of what was to become his recurrent illness. Two years later he made final revisions to the score and considered using the mass to support his application for a post at court, which also came to nothing. The original composition of the fifth mass in November 1819 (D678) was contemporary with another sacred work for similar forces, *Lazarus*, an Easter Oratorio intended to be in three acts (D689). It was similarly set aside, and like most of the works not immediately completed, was never finished. Despite this, the first two acts were performed under Ferdinand in Schubert's lifetime; and the work has been revived and performed in 1863, and again for the centenary in 1928.

THE MASSES AND THE OPERAS 179

The final Mass in E flat, composed only months before Schubert's death, is the most substantial of the works of that final year and the greatest of the masses. As we have seen, for much of the 20th century it was accepted that the *Great* C Major Symphony was also written in that same miraculous year. Whilst now known to date from some 3 years earlier, it beggars belief that no one questioned how two such major works could have been composed in the same year, especially given the other works that appeared in 1828. Schubert died before he was able to hear the final mass, which was performed the following year, on 4 October 1829, under the direction of his brother Ferdinand. This great work and the earlier masses, and sacred works, continued to be heard in churches in Vienna and in other cities.

One performance was heard by Ferdinand, who wrote to his brother recounting a visit to Pressburg in 1824. Ferdinand had been invited to a local church where his host explained that a mass was to be given 'by a well-known and famous composer – only I can't think of his name at the moment.' It turned out to be the Mass No 3 in B flat.* The masses and other sacred works have continued to be given in many churches and in many countries as they continue to be heard today. Performances of the sacred works, especially the larger masses, are also regularly given in concert halls throughout Europe and beyond. They have been an important vehicle for conveying Schubert's name and fame from Vienna to the rest of the western world and contain within their pages an important element of the composer's output, ranging almost from first to last. For an account of the masses and other sacred works in the context of Schubert's other compositions and development, see *Franz Schubert: Music and Belief by Leo Black.*†

An issue which could possibly have held back the masses from being performed was Schubert's personal re-rendering of

---

* Deutsch: *Docs*, letter 6 October 1824, No 500.
† Boydel Press 2003.

the traditional text, removing lines from the *Gloria* and *Credo*, which appear in each of the works. This did not deter Viennese congregations during the composer's lifetime, but increasing theological concern led, in 1897 (perhaps in anticipation of greater use of the works), to a papal ban on liturgical use of the masses, a ban which was removed only later in the twentieth century.

THE OPERAS

Schubert began to write operas at the very start of his composing career, the first of these being the unfinished *Der Spiegelritter* (D11) in 1811. He continued to write stage works of which a substantial proportion remained unfinished up to late 1823, with a final burst of activity in 1827. There were therefore no 'late' operas and no equivalent to the final Mass in E flat. His total output for the stage comprised some 18 works, including *Singspiele* and plays with incidental music. The stage works comprise the largest section of the collected works, occupying seven volumes. Notwithstanding this output, only eight were completed and ready for the stage. And of those eight only three were performed in the composer's lifetime.

The list of Schubert's operas and their fate is well documented and can be related shortly. Thanks to the patronage of Vogl, the Kärntnertor Theater put on, in June 1820, Hofmann's play *Die Zwillingsbrüder* (D647) with Schubert's incidental music. The opera has a fine overture and, as the title suggests, concerns twin brothers who lead separate lives but which eventually coincide, leading to mistaken identities and love matches with the wrong brother. The first and only production ran for a total of six performances, with Vogl taking the parts of both brothers. This was the first production of any of Schubert's stage works despite his having by then composed some nine works, most of which were not completed. The immediate attraction of Schubert's music led to a commission by the same theatre for the three-act play, also by Hofmann, *Die Zauberharfe* (D644), which later the same year achieved eight performances. It must be said that from this point onwards it was clear that Schubert's choice of libretti would be a potential stumbling block to any lasting popularity. *Die Zwillingsbrüder* was at best marginally plausible but the plot of *Die Zauberharfe* was worse and entirely trivial, concerning a magic harp, with little to recommend it save some fine individual numbers. It was very far from a *Magic Flute*.

However, buoyed up by this limited initial success Schubert, in the following year 1821 and in the company of von Schober as librettist, embarked on the full-scale opera *Alfonso und Estrella* (D732), the story of which has been summarised in Chapter 7. This grand opera was completed in 1822 but was notoriously passed over in favour of the current fad for Italian opera. It was destined never to receive a performance in Schubert's lifetime despite serious attempts and promises. The plot created many difficulties for a production, but the real reason for it being rejected was the competition from Rossini.

It was later, in early 1823, that Schubert became seriously ill and was forced to return to the family home. Undeterred, he continued with operas, composing a one-act *Singspiel Die Verschworenen* (D787) with a libretto by Castelli based on a light-hearted Greek play, the *Lysistrata* of Aristophanes, with Greek warriors being translated into medieval Austrian knights. This was followed by a three-act opera to a play by Josef Kupelwieser (brother of the painter), *Fierrabras* (D796). This was perhaps the most easily accessible of the operas, based on tales of Frankish chivalry. The plot concerns wars in medieval Spain between the Franks and the Moors, the title role being given to a Moorish prince who is intent on renouncing his religion. After much fighting the parties reach a truce and Roland, the captured commander of the Franks, is released and reunited with Florinda, the daughter of the Moorish prince, with *Fierrabras* now joining the ranks of the Frankish king. Finally, in 1823 Schubert composed the extensive incidental music to the play

Rosamunde, Fürstin von Cypern (D797), using the overture to *Alfonso und Estrella*, now better known as the *Rosamunde* overture.

The Rosamunde of the title role is a princess of Cyprus who has been brought up as a shepherdess, but upon regaining her proper status, she and her prince undergo many trials before being finally united. The play, with Schubert's music, enjoyed successful but limited performances in December 1823, after which the orchestral parts were neatly tied up and placed in store from which, as we have seen, they were recovered by George Grove and Arthur Sullivan in 1867. Despite spending time in 1827 on another projected grand opera, *Der Graf von Gleichen* (D918), with a libretto by Schubert's dramatist friend Eduard von Bauernfeld, the work was never completed nor any of it performed. Schubert himself spent time and energy trying to secure performances for his operas elsewhere than Vienna, and there were promises to promote *Alfonso und Estrella* in Graz by Karl Pachler and *Fierrabras* in Berlin by Anna Fröhlich. However all this came to nothing during the composer's lifetime.

POSTHUMOUS PRODUCTIONS

Only after Schubert's death were some of the unperformed operas and *Singspiele* finally heard, including a number of early and unfinished works, beginning with numbers from *Fernando* (D220) and *Fierrabras* (D796) in 1830 and 1835. Then, after a long period of silence, an edited version of *Alfonso und Estrella* was performed in Weimar in 1854, conducted by Liszt, for whom Schober, the now maligned librettist, worked as a secretary. Liszt, having studied the work, regarded the poor libretto as a major drawback to the opera's promotion and reportedly considered employing a ghostwriter to recompose the libretto, but this was abandoned in favour of editing.

In the 1860s, when the revival of interest in the composer and his compositions was gathering pace, a concert version of *Die Verschworenen* (D787) was given in Vienna, together with numbers from the unperformed *Der Graf von Gleichen* (D918) and *Adrast* (D137), on 1 March 1861. In the following decade numbers from *Die Freunde von Salamanka* (D326) and *Des Teufels Lustschloss* (D84) were heard, and a staged performance of *Fierrabras* (D796) was given in Schubert's centenary year of 1897 in Karlsruhe. The period up to the First World War saw concert versions of *Fernando* (D220), *Die Bürgschaft* (D435) and *Claudine von Villa Bella* (D239), all in Vienna. Subsequently, performances of the unfinished *Der Spiegelritter* (D11) and *Sakuntala* (D701) took place. In more modern times, the first fully staged performance of *Fierrabras* was given in Vienna in 1988 at the Theater an der Wien, conducted by Claudio Abbado and with Thomas Hampson in the title role. The production was recorded by Deutsche Grammaphon and remains available.

Several of the operas have been produced in England and by English companies abroad, notably *Fierrabras* at the Buxton Festival in 2000, and festival performances of *Alfonso und Estrella* by Opéra de Baugé in Anjou, Loire, in 2019. Productions continue in many venues as the fashion for hitherto unheard operas gains force. However, the level of public and even academic interest in this major genre of Schubert's output falls far short of the attention given to almost every other area of his compositions and gives rise to many questions for Schubert enthusiasts.

SCHUBERT'S AMBITION

Schubert remained convinced throughout his active life, or at least up to 1827, his final attempt at opera composition, that the path to success as a composer was through the opera house. This was hardly surprising given the career and works of Gluck, Mozart, Haydn, and even Beethoven. Schubert is said to have sold his school books to buy a ticket to the first performance of the final version of *Fidelio*, which took place on 23 May 1814, after which Schubert was motivated to revise his own early opera *Des Teufels Lustschloss* which was, however, not to be performed until long after his death.

Of the other opera composers of the day, Donizetti was an exact contemporary but visited Vienna only after Schubert's death. Rossini, five years Schubert's senior, not only visited Vienna but reputedly had an interview with the now deaf Beethoven in 1822. It was the Viennese preference for Rossini, and for Italian rather than German opera, that effectively sabotaged Schubert's efforts to get his own opera *Fierrabras* performed in 1823. Schubert well knew of Rossini and his works, and Rossini was no doubt also aware of Schubert's music and growing reputation. Schubert, in response to Rossini's appearance on the musical scene, had already in 1817 composed two witty overtures *In the Italian Style* (D590, 591). However, there is neither record nor even suggestion of any meeting between the two.

What other opera composers, as well as the musical public of Vienna, sadly missed, was the contribution to operatic development that Schubert's works could have brought about, had they been heard and appreciated. In a review of the stage works for the *Schubert Symposium* edited by Gerald Abraham,* Hyatt King offers the following comment on the score of *Fierrabras*:

> Schubert's orchestration with the aid of the leitmotive make him worthy of a far more prominent place in the history of operatic development than has ever been accorded to him.

Thomas A. Denny, in a critical review of the full opera output in the *Cambridge Companion to Schubert*† concludes that:

---

* *Schubert Symposium*, ed Abraham, 1946, p 210.
† *Cambridge Companion*, 1997, p 224.

It is enough to acknowledge that *Fierrabras* deserves a spot on the periphery of the standard repertory. It is enough that we set aside the lingering generalisations that Schubert was an inept opera composer.

Maurice Brown in his entry in the *New Grove Dictionary* of 1980 pursues the issue with more enthusiasm, describing the works in these terms:

> from *Des Teufels Lustschloss* (D84) to the final operas there is a clear evolution of his operatic style: the music grows in colour, fluidity and scope. It is unlike the evolution of his songs or instrumental work; it belongs entirely to this unknown sphere of his music. There is an extended use, for example, of richly accompanied recitative, which is quite his own; figuration grows more complex and weaves between voice and orchestra … in a manner quite unlike anything in the songs … . His handling of the orchestra, competent in *Lustschloss*, grows in skill and boldness until it has the true Schubertian quality, known chiefly from the *Rosamunde* music and the last two symphonies, a quality which was … the outcome of his endless experimentation and exploration of possibilities in the operas.

In no sense can these works be seen as music best overlooked and forgotten. But they still await a proper introduction to the musical repertoire and the level of attention, both academic and commercial, that is lavished on the more popular end of Schubert's huge output. They should at least be afforded the same respectful attention as the masses. Fortunately, while the operas still lack the resources and support necessary to mount productions, this has not deterred performances of the music, of which there is now scarcely a bar that has not been recorded, and which is now accessible via the many media sources available to electronic devices, including mobile phones. Anyone who wishes to sample any of the operas now has many hours of pleasure awaiting them.

LILAC TIME

An event of supreme irony, if not duplicity, took place in wartime Vienna in 1916 when an operetta titled *Das Dreimäderlhaus* (House of Three Girls), was staged with huge success. The work was based on the plot of a novella entitled *Schwammerl* (Schubert's affectionate nickname, meaning 'little mushroom') by R. H. Bartsch and adapted for the stage by A. M. Willner and Heinz Reichert. The work, crucially, borrowed freely from Schubert's music – not his operatic music but a free mixture of his most popular melodies from all sources including *lieder* and piano works. The production was a huge success and left any of the original performances of Schubert's operas, during or after his lifetime to that date, well in the shade.

So successful was the production that, after the war, it was adapted and performed on Broadway in New York in September 1921 with the title *Blossom Time* and at the Lyric Theatre, London, in December 1922 under the title by which it is still well known in England: *Lilac Time*. Advertisements for the production latched on to the currently fashionable depiction of Schubert as a handsome and smartly dressed young man about town.

The plot, which owes something to Edmond Rostand's Cyrano de Bergerac, concerns a shy young composer (Franz Schubert, of course) who writes a beautiful love song to his beloved Mitzi. But he gets his best friend Baron Schober (the original von Schober was indeed a baron) to sing it to her.

She, naturally, falls in love with him instead of poor Franz, who has to find consolation in their happiness. Subplots concern Mitzi's two sisters and their lovers as well as other typical Viennese characters. Such was the success that the work was adapted and further arranged for successive productions, including versions for amateur performances. It continued in the repertory at least until the 1960s by which time it is estimated to have notched up more than 85,000 performances worldwide.

Schubert appearing in *Lilac Time*

POSTSCRIPT

The irony is that Schubert never intended to write for this market, which did not even exist in the 1820s. His sights were set on a higher objective, seeking to create in his operas works of unified dramatic and musical narrative. The duplicity was in picking from wholly disconnected works what an undiscerning public would lap up, because the tunes were already familiar. However, we should not be too dismissive of the work, seeing how popular the music obviously was, and is today – it even forms the subject of academic study.*

Concert promoters in the nineteenth century saw nothing objectionable in mixing works, even to the extent of interposing pieces of light relief between movements of heavier moment by composers who otherwise deserved more respect, including Beethoven. So the question is whether the attraction of *Lilac Time* could be more usefully directed towards bringing more of Schubert's operatic output into the public consciousness. Perhaps Liszt's original idea of having the libretto of *Alfonso und Estrella* recomposed had merit. And in any event there should be no qualms about performing arrangements and selections from the operas as an alternative to hearing the full operas, whose time, it seems, is still to come.

Thus we have seen how two of the major genres of Schubert's output – the sacred works and the operas, which occupied an important part of his musical ambitions – were received by the musical public both in Schubert's day and subsequently in very different ways. While their musical merits must be on comparable levels, the masses have been universally accepted, regularly performed and admired, while the operas and other dramatic works have been substantially sidelined, even in the current climate of increased levels of academic research. The merits of the operas at least deserve more respectful attention.

---

* Reportedly at the University of Leeds and elsewhere.

CHAPTER 17
THE SYMPHONIES

Schubert is currently credited with 10 symphonies, a number that has steadily, but perhaps not surprisingly, grown in the years since the manuscripts began to emerge shortly after his death. An early fragment of a single symphonic movement, probably of 1811, has been added, but has not disturbed the now generally accepted numbering. We have seen already that seven completed symphonies were known to Ferdinand, who had custody of most of the scores from shortly after his brother's death, which occurred in his own apartment. The last of these, then given the number seven, is the *Great* C Major which created its own aura of greatness following its 'discovery' by Schumann and subsequent performance and publication after the enthusiastic intervention of Mendelssohn, all in 1839. This symphony, as we have seen, was well known to Ferdinand who had himself copied out the score, leaving the original, bearing Schubert's manuscript changes, safely in the library of the Gesellschaft der Musikfreunde in Vienna. Ferdinand had also in his possession the four movement manuscript sketch of the Symphony in E Major which has generated much interest and attention as well as some controversy. That symphony is generally now referred to as No 7* so that, after the rediscovery of the *Unfinished* as No 8, the *Great* C Major Symphony was reassigned to its now permanent place as No 9.

The so-called *Unfinished* Symphony – No 8 – has, since its rediscovery and impact on the musical world from December 1865, become possibly the most widely performed and universally loved symphony in the whole classical repertoire. In addition to these familiar works the list must now include the tenth, a substantially unscored sketch symphony found among Schubert's last manuscripts at his death. These two works, now bearing their correct numbers, eight and ten, have each attracted attention and study from generations of scholars seeking, as we have seen, to complete the uncompleted or at least to present to the listening public that which might have been, had Schubert himself completed their composition.

To this list can now be added, after the painstaking research devoted to the collection and publication of the complete works in the two decades following the re-emergence of the *Unfinished*, two additional (un-numbered) symphonic fragments, composed in 1820 and 1821. The first comprises two movements as a fragmentary piano sketch in D Major catalogued as D615; and the second a four-movement fragmentary sketch catalogued as D708A. Both have been the subject of more recent academic study. Their interest lies, in particular, in their being positioned immediately before Symphony No 7 (D729) and the *Unfinished* (D759) and thus having been composed on the verge of Schubert's maturity and the advent of some of his greatest works.

THE FIRST SIX SYMPHONIES REDISCOVERED

The symphonies one to six, unlike the works that were to follow,

---

* It is of some note that the German-speaking world generally does not recognise the manuscript Symphony in E as meriting a number, with the consequence that the *Unfinished* becomes No 7 and the *Great* C Major No 8.

are all complete and each has four conventional movements. They are all neatly and fully scored for a variety of musical forces, no doubt reflecting what was available at the time of composition. It is no exaggeration to say that they have received only scant attention over the two centuries since they were written and continue to be regarded as somewhat minor works, written in preparation for the much greater works of the 1820s. The earlier symphonies were all composed between 1813 and 1818 and thus span the later years of his formal education, the ill-fated attempt to turn him in to a schoolmaster and his escape to the Bohemian life as a freelance composer.

During these years the young composer was producing many of his early masterpieces in the fields of *lieder*, masses, piano works – including dances and chamber music – as well as orchestral overtures. How is it then that the early works of Mozart and the unpublished works of Beethoven are so revered and yet the early symphonies of Schubert still command relatively little attention? This was certainly the position back in 1835 when Ferdinand offered seven symphonies as part of the package of works available for performance 'at moderate fees.' As we have seen the only taker, after the passage of more than four years, was Robert Schumann, who examined many of the works in Ferdinand's famous chest and selected the *Great* C Major Symphony for transmission to Mendelssohn and the beginning of its journey to eventual worldwide acclaim. Yet the other six symphonies were of little or no interest despite Ferdinand dispatching the manuscript of No 6 to Leipzig along with the *Great* C Major. Could it be that Schumann, himself still establishing a reputation as a composer, thought one symphony was enough and did not want to be overwhelmed by six more? Whatever the explanation, the six remained in obscurity for several more decades after the emergence of the *Great* C Major and after the deaths of both Schumann and Mendelssohn, and then Ferdinand himself.

So it was that George Grove and Arthur Sullivan, in search of hitherto unknown Schubert manuscripts, were to examine the collection which had by then been inherited from Ferdinand, on his death, by Schubert's lawyer nephew, Dr Schneider. Here they were to discover a treasure trove which included the early symphonies, of whose existence they had only the vaguest knowledge. Grove's journey to Vienna took place shortly after he had received and heard the *Unfinished* Symphony at the Crystal Palace in April 1867. This had naturally whetted his appetite for what still might be discovered and the Vienna trip was planned for October of that year. Once in Vienna Grove records that:

> I eagerly asked everyone whom I met – Mr Joachim, Madame Schumann, and others – for information as to the rest of the symphonies, but without success; no one had seen them or knew anything about them.

Then came the visit to the office of Dr Schneider where the visitors were able to examine five of the six symphonies as now known, and to make copies of the music. The details of the visit are conveniently published as the Appendix to the English translation of von Hellborn's biography. Of some interest are the remarks on Symphony No 5, which has proved to be the most popular of the six early symphonies. The manuscript of No 5 was not forthcoming, but a copy of the score and the orchestral parts were found to be in the possession of the Musikverein and in the safekeeping of Mr Herbeck (who had played a central role in the rescue and subsequent performance of the *Unfinished* Symphony). The copy finally examined by Grove had reportedly been made by Ferdinand. The explanation, as revealed by Maurice Brown,* is that Ferdinand had in 1842 (after Schumann's visit and his lack of interest in the early symphonies) sold the manuscript of No 5 to a Leipzig publisher (Whistling). They passed on the manuscript, which was eventually acquired

---

* M. Brown, *A Critical Biography* p 62.

by the Preussische Staatsbibliothek, Berlin, and the Deutsch thematic catalogue states that the copy was not by Ferdinand. Whether No 5 was performed in Leipzig or in Berlin is not recorded, but it is known that piano duet versions of the symphonies were published and therefore doubtless performed. But none of this was to lead to symphonies gaining any degree of popularity; and it was Grove's obtaining copies of the scores in 1867 which led to the first public performances of the symphonies in London in the following years.

Grove's notes also include a summary of the sketch of Symphony No 7 which had been presented by Ferdinand to Mendelssohn and which, by 1867, had been presented back to Grove by Mendelssohn's brother Paul.* So far as the von Hellborn biography deals with the symphonies, the greatest service was to record the existence of the Symphony in B Minor of 1822, of which Josef Hüttenbrenner is recorded as stating that his brother Anselm 'has the original score' and that there were no other copies in existence. Publication of this information was enough to send Johann von Herbeck post haste to Graz where he was able to recover the manuscript and see that the work was given back to the public from whom it had been concealed for too long. As regards the *Great* C Major Symphony, whilst it was by 1863 known and performed internationally, von Hellborn confines his observation to the (misleading) date on the original manuscript and records that in early 1828 'The completion of his symphony in C enabled him to give convincing proof of what he could do with grand orchestral works ... .' As regards the remaining six earlier symphonies, von Hellborn says little and records simply in his list of unpublished works, the existence of six symphonies, all of which are said (inaccurately as discovered by Grove) to be in Dr Schneider's possession.

---

* The manuscript was given by Grove to the Royal College of Music of which he became the first principal.

THE SYMPHONIES PERFORMED

The question of where and when these early symphonies were originally performed remains uncertain, with the exception of Nos 5 and 6 which are specifically recalled in a memoir of 1868 by Leopold von Sonnleithner as having been performed by the amateur orchestra in which Schubert himself played the viola. The Sixth Symphony, which became known as the 'Little C Major' was in circulation in 1828 when Schubert himself suggested its substitution for the *Great* C Major in the concert planned for December 1828, and which in fact took place after the composer's death. As to the rest, they were without doubt performed by amateur orchestras in which Schubert played or which he directed, at the school or in later orchestras as recorded.

We have seen the agonising birth pangs of the *Great* C Major Symphony which the Musikfreunde, after rewarding the composer for the dedication, arranged to perform, and for this purpose prepared the orchestral parts. But a rebellion by the orchestra led to Schubert proposing the substitution of the 'Little C Major' symphony, No 6, which was, in the event, performed at the concert given after Schubert's death. This episode at least tells us something of Schubert's own opinion of No 6 which, although composed 10 years earlier and not of the same breadth and grandeur as the *Great* C Major, was nevertheless a work which the composer was prepared to put forward to demonstrate his abilities to the Viennese public.

Performances of the *Unfinished* posed no such problems. After it was first performed under Johann von Herbeck in 1865 in Vienna, the symphony was taken up by others, reaching London in 1867. There were, of course, reasons why the *Unfinished* was not performed for well over four decades after its composition. Not so with the first six symphonies, however, which despite Ferdinand's valiant attempts to gain recognition, remained unnoticed and, as we have seen, virtually unknown until Grove's rediscovery in 1867. Once they had emerged it was Grove and Augustus Manns in London who performed the works, all six being heard between 1867 and 1881 including almost certainly the world premiere of Nos 1, 2 and 3 since the composer's lifetime. After that time, performances of the first six symphonies, with the possible exception of No 5, have become comparatively rare in the world's concert halls, at least until the last few years. The point is made in rather brutal fashion in Donald Tovey's essay,* where the great musicologist gives the following summary of the early symphonies:

> Schubert's mature symphonic style is represented by one and a half symphonies ... . If we explore the other symphonies of Schubert we must be prepared for a kind of stiff Mozartian style, charming in itself and frequently foreshadowing the great Schubert in passages mostly pretty and quaint, but occasionally suggestive of deeper thoughts. Yet suggestions and foreshadowings are all that we shall get, and we shall fail to represent Schubert's mature orchestral ideas.

This may well summarise why performances of the early symphonies were a comparative rarity. But in the decades that have followed Tovey, different views have emerged, particularly given the ease with which recordings can now be made accessible, without the need to satisfy the eternally conservative taste of concertgoers. The result has been a willingness to experiment and to explore in more depth Schubert's intentions in the early symphonies and to present the music not as some pale derivative of his great predecessors and contemporaries, but as Schubert's own musical language, to stand alongside his other masterpieces of the time. As proof of the emergence of a new appreciation of these early works they are today increasingly

---

* *A Schubert Centenary Concert*, 1928.

appearing in concert programmes.* And within the same timeframe the celebrated orchestras and conductors have seen fit to revisit these symphonies and to discover new qualities, seemingly belied by Tovey and his generation.†

In addition, performances have included the symphonies left only as sketches. In particular the sketched Symphony in E Major, properly referred to as No 7, was completed in full orchestral score by J. F. Barnett and performed in 1883. Since then, despite Barnett's score being lost, alternative completions have appeared and performances of the work can now be accessed in several versions. Likewise, the fragmentary works of 1820 and 1821 and of the Tenth Symphony can all be readily accessed in recorded completions. In the case of No 10, two versions have received critical attention. First a conventional completion by Brian Newbould, which demonstrates the new ideas that were forming in the composer's mind even as he approached his end. Following this version, a very different work was composed by Luciano Berio in which Schubert's sketched ideas are incorporated into a fantasia, with Schubert's music being heard as though from a distance in time and space.

THE MUSIC

The repertoire starts with Symphony No 1, composed in 1813 between leaving the seminary and starting at the teacher training college. The work is naturally reminiscent of Haydn, Mozart and Beethoven, but only in the sense that each of these reminds us of the others. Schubert's symphony, in the words of Maurice Brown in 1958, was 'completely individual in content;' it is tender, intimate and full of musical fancy in which we hear his voice alone. As noted, the First Symphony, as D82, was preceded by the

---

* The first six symphonies have, since at least 2010, been regularly performed at the BBC Proms.
† The latest of these, the so-called B'Rock (Beyond Baroque) Orchestra founded in Belgium by the Scholar René Jacobs, has recorded all the early symphonies.

sketch of 1811, given the number D2B. Both are in the key of D Major, the key of Beethoven's Second Symphony which Schubert greatly admired. The sketch is reproduced by Brian Newbould,* who points out the connections to both works. But curiously the sketch, which is scored for full orchestra, includes three trombones, a feature of Schubert's later works, particularly in Symphonies 7, 8 and 9, but one not used in any of the earlier symphonies. Nor were trombones used by Beethoven before the Fifth Symphony of 1805. Was Schubert ahead of his time or anticipating the wonderful orchestral scoring still to come?

The next four symphonies were composed over a span of only two years, 1814 to 1816. They are, again in the words of Maurice Brown, unmistakably the work of an original artist; neither immature nor imitative, containing vital melodic charm and 'their varied harmony and their orchestral fancy give them an appeal which is often lacking in the mature symphonies of other composers.' Dvořák was an ardent admirer of Schubert and while deploring the neglect of the symphonies in the 1890s, proudly related the many times he had conducted the works. No 5 has become a particular favourite but all the symphonies maintain the charm and freshness of their first performances during the composer's lifetime, and subsequently their resurrection courtesy of George Grove and Augustus Manns in the 1870s. Sadly, the resurrection was not to be sustained and also was not helped by the observations of Donald Tovey in 1928. But as already noted, a more recent and one hopes permanent resurrection is now underway, propelled by the recording industry and other more far-seeing performers and conductors.

Finally, of the early symphonies, No 6 was started in October 1817 but not completed until February 1818, by Schubert's standards an unusually long period. The work shows great technical advances and is recognised as a turning point both in Schubert's life and his music. In the case of the former, he had abandoned

---

* B. Newbould, *Schubert and the Symphony*, p 25.

his teaching career and was now dependent for his livelihood on composing. As to the latter, the work had left the charmed and charming world of the earlier symphonies and, as noted by many commentators, had reverted more closely to the lessons of his revered Beethoven and of Haydn. The work is said not to have been a favourite of Schubert but, as we have seen, was nominated by Schubert himself as the substitute for the projected performance of the *Great* C Major in 1828, which proved to be beyond the capability of the orchestra. The development in Schubert's music between 1818, which marked his 21st birthday, and 1822, the year of the *Unfinished* Symphony represents, in the view of many commentators, the advent of his true stature and greatness. In terms of the symphonies it is represented first by No 6 and then by three attempts at a new symphonic approach, each left unfinished to different degrees.

THE TURNING POINT

While Symphony No 6 was the beginning of a transition, the process was to continue through to the composition of Tovey's 'one-and-a-half' great symphonies after only a few months' pause. In May 1818, the two movement piano sketch (D615) in D was written, but then abandoned; and after a further pause of over a year, a further four-movement piano sketch, also in D, was produced (D708A) but also abandoned. These sketches appeared only during the systematic collection of the whole of Schubert's vast output and were unknown to earlier scholars. Indeed, D708A eluded even Deutsch's catalogue. These works in any event existed only as sketches, inaccessible to any but the skilled musicologist and then only as manuscripts. Happily both works have been brought to life by Brian Newbould in arrangements for full orchestra, as intended or implied from the piano score. These have now been recorded making it possible to hear what, up to now, only Schubert had heard in his mind, and to appreciate the great developments in the composer's approach to symphonic writing at this turning point in his compositions. Newbould presents his analysis of the works* along with his account of transforming the piano sketches into orchestral scores. The analysis reveals flaws which may account for the abandonment of both works, but also recognises some parts as 'very promising indeed.' Of particular interest is the Scherzo third movement of D708A in which Schubert writes a four-part fugal exposition, for the first time in any of his symphonies, in which he demonstrates great contrapuntal ingenuity. Fugal writing can also be seen in the final movement of the *Great* C Major Symphony, surely giving the lie to any suggestion that he had anything to learn from the teaching of Simon Sechter in the last weeks of his life.

The third unfinished work, and the last before composition of the *Unfinished* Symphony, is the fully worked out four-movement orchestral sketch, now designated Symphony No 7 of 1821 (D729). It was this bound manuscript that Ferdinand sent to Mendelssohn as a gift, in recognition (and relief) following his efforts to realise and perform the *Great* C Major Symphony in Leipzig in 1839. It was Mendelssohn's letter of thanks to Ferdinand that referred to the uncompleted manuscript as having allowed him to '[get] to know your brother personally.'† As we have seen, by 1867 Grove had recovered the manuscript from Mendelssohn's brother and was thus able to include in his synopsis of Schubert's hitherto unknown works, a summary of the four movements of D729. Grove added that

> Mr Sullivan has played it through to me on the piano and I am allowed by him to say that in quality it appears to be inferior to none of its predecessors, and to abound in beauties; which I do, earnestly trusting that some means may before long be found of restoring this lost treasure to the world.

---

* Newbould, *Schubert and the Symphony*, Chapter X.
† See further, in Chapter 5.

Grove's wishes were not in vain as today at least three full completions of the symphony exist; the first being by the English musicologist John Francis Barnett in 1881, followed by Felix Weingartner in 1934 and Brian Newbould in 1980. The full story of the rebirth and life of Symphony No 7 has been told by the late Stan Freed in *The Schubertian** which discloses the many adventures associated with the symphony which, happily, is now freely available in a number of recordings. Brian Newbould summarises the effect of the work as follows: 'The seventh provides a fascinating link, reflecting the familiar middle-period Schubert, assimilating (especially in its themes) his current interest in Rossini, and anticipating – in its transitions rather than its themes, but not exclusively so – several facets of the sound-world to come in the imminent masterpieces of the fully mature symphonist.'

The rest of the story of Schubert's symphonies can be related shortly, as the two great parts of Tovey's 'one-and-a-half symphonies' have been dealt with earlier in their historical context. The *Unfinished*, No 8, was also the *unknown* until Josef Hüttenbrenner was shamed into passing on information as to its whereabouts (and indeed its existence) to von Hellborn, after which its progress became unstoppable and remains so today. The existence of No 9, the *Great* C Major, was well known but it remained unheard after its completion, and during the last three years of the composer's life, despite one attempt at performance. It then disappeared into Ferdinand's famous chest, despite his attempts to bring it to the world's attention, until rescued by a chance meeting with Robert Schumann; and the rest is history.

These two great works are properly regarded as the pinnacle of Schubert's mature or 'middle' period of symphonic writing. What might have followed was another even more radical work now known as the Tenth Symphony already described. This can also be easily accessed in the completed and recorded versions

---

* *The Schubertian* (SIUK), editions of 2020.

which have only been available in recent years. But rather than speculate, we should be persuaded to go back to the earlier, fully completed symphonies which have been shamefully neglected, like so much else of the huge output of this great and enigmatic genius.

PART V EPILOGUE

CHAPTER 18
SCHUBERT AND OTHER COMPOSERS

Schubert was born into a world of music, at home, at school and seemingly in the air of Vienna, where messenger boys were reputed to have whistled the latest tunes from *Figaro*. He was acutely aware of the great masters who preceded him, not least those with recent connections to Vienna, and was brought up studying and performing their music. Some still see Schubert as a pale imitation of Beethoven and Mozart, who developed but failed to live up to their legacies. His connections with those who preceded him and those who were to follow is therefore an important part of the story of Franz Schubert, which seeks to show that the reverse is the case.

INFLUENCE OF OTHER COMPOSERS

How far was Schubert influenced by other composers? This is not a difficult question since Schubert was brought up in the city of Mozart and Haydn; and while Mozart had died six years before Schubert's birth Haydn, now in his sixties, was still living and working in Vienna up to Schubert's eleventh year. The symphonies and other works of these two great masters were the staple fare at the Stadtkonvikt, where the orchestra, in which his close friend Josef von Spaun played, and in which Schubert took an increasingly prominent role, regularly performed their works and, to keep up with current trends, those of Beethoven too. So it was inevitable that the budding composer from the age of 12 or 13 should adopt a style of composition which, superficially, is easily mistaken for one of these great role models. Today the cognoscenti will detect, from the First Symphony of 1813 (D82) onwards, Schubert's original musical ideas, but this was not always so. As his musical education progressed Schubert, as we have seen, studied with Salieri who exposed him to Italian opera and oratorio. But it is of some interest that from the start of Schubert's vocal writing, including the many *lieder* but exemplified in his first Mass in F (D105) of 1814, the style is Schubert's own, and with no detectable Italian influence. His vocal works, from the start, are unlikely to be mistaken for those of any other composer.

There is no denying the huge influence that Beethoven had on Schubert, and the struggle involved in establishing his unique artistic personality while working alongside the towering example of the man whose works Schubert revered above all others. He had taken part in performances of Beethoven's earlier symphonies at the seminary and would have acquired an intimate knowledge of the scores. Beethoven's orchestral works at this time were popular in Vienna and were performed regularly. Schubert heard many of them at public concerts, in addition to his studies of the works. He was particularly influenced by the Seventh Symphony, references to which can be heard in his own music, but by way of respectful admiration and not mere imitation. And as we shall see, as Schubert became more confident in his own style of composing, he was not averse to a little gentle mocking of the works of his great mentor.

The six early symphonies which Schubert wrote between 1813 and 1818 were all in the classical mode of these masters, albeit clearly the product of a new and fresh mind. They did not attempt to emulate the daring innovations of the later Beethoven symphonies; and when Schubert came to compose his two greatest symphonies, the *Unfinished* in 1822 and the *Great* C Major in 1825, the music was pure and original Schubert, who was by then travelling his own unique road. The same remarks could be made about the later string quartets and piano sonatas: when Schubert composed his mature works they were new and original creations of a composer, today seen as standing on the same pedestal as his own great hero. In the field of *lieder*, while Beethoven did compose one notable song cycle and a number of other songs, his *lieder* cannot be seen as heralding Schubert's outpourings in the genre, which were of unprecedented originality and variety and unsurpassed either before or after his lifetime.

ENCOUNTERS IN SCHUBERT'S LIFETIME

Did Schubert meet Beethoven? There seems no doubt that the elder composer was aware of Schubert's highly original and growing volume of *lieder* and cannot have failed to detect the spark of genius. However many other budding composers might have sought his patronage. An incident is related by Anton Schindler, Beethoven's companion and first biographer, from early 1827 and presumably before Beethoven was on his deathbed. Schindler recalled having taken copies of a substantial number of Schubert's songs to present to Beethoven, who examined them and expressed enthusiastic approval. A much earlier incident is recorded in 1818 concerning Schubert's dedication of a set of Piano Variations (D624), for which Beethoven had granted permission. Josef Hüttenbrenner recalled (in 1858) that Beethoven played the Variations almost every day with his nephew, Karl. Neither of the Hüttenbrenners (Josef or his brother Anselm) can be regarded as reliable witnesses regarding Schubert's life. But whatever the truth of this event, it can safely be concluded that Beethoven was well aware of Schubert's compositions and was surely in a position, like no other critic, to assess their true merit. Ironically it was not until 1822 that the Variations, even with the dedication to Beethoven, were published as Opus 10.

Quite apart from any meeting, it is clear that Schubert was acutely aware of Beethoven's popularity and of particular pieces of his music which everyone in Vienna would be familiar with, such as the famous opening bars of the Fifth Symphony and later the equally famous *Ode to Joy* set in the final movement of the Ninth Symphony. So much so it is not surprising that Schubert should indulge in a gentle piece of parody, as though saying to those paying sufficiently close attention, 'See what I can do with the same material?' Anyone in the first decades of the nineteenth century, hearing the opening of Schubert's *Death and the Maiden* Quartet, with a long note followed by a triplet, both repeated, could not be unaware that Schubert had reversed the dramatic opening sequence of the Fifth Symphony, and even followed this up with two more repeats with the triplet preceding the long note. It is, of course, an open question whether what Schubert then did with the material surpassed Beethoven's treatment of it.

The other obvious example is in the finale of Schubert's *Great* C Major Symphony, where some bars of the finale of the Choral Symphony are suddenly quoted by Schubert and then developed as part of his final movement, ending as we know with the triumphal finale of that notable work. The *Great* C Major was written probably within a year of the concert in May 1824 in which the Choral Symphony was first heard, and to any listener would have been an obvious quotation. But of course Schubert's symphony was heard by no-one until 1839 and is it doubtful if anyone, 14 years later and in Leipzig, would have made the connection.

The opening of the development section in the finale of the *Great* C Major Symphony where a pair of clarinets in E flat give out the theme from Beethoven's Choral Symphony

BEETHOVEN, HUMMEL AND WEBER

During the final weeks of Beethoven's life, in March 1827, there are several different accounts of a visit to pay homage to the great composer who was then known to be on his deathbed. There is no reliable source and no record from Schubert himself of such an event. However, the fact that others are known to have visited the deathbed and that Schubert is said to have made the visit accompanied by a group of friends makes it more likely the visit did happen. If it did, it is most unlikely that any communication took place between the two composers, given Schubert's reticence and Beethoven's extreme condition. Bearing in mind that Beethoven was, in any event, stone deaf and communicated only through a notebook, it is most unlikely that he uttered the prophetic words about Schubert's 'divine spark.' In retrospect there was no need anyway.

Another visitor to Beethoven's deathbed, in March 1827, was Johann Nepomuk Hummel, celebrated *Kapellmeister*, virtuoso and composer, who had travelled from Weimar to renew his longstanding friendship with Beethoven. After Beethoven's death Hummel, along with Schubert, was a mourner at the funeral. While in Vienna, Hummel was invited to attend a Schubertiad at which Vogl and Schubert performed numerous songs. These are said to have deeply impressed the visitor, who had previously been unaware of Schubert's existence. Hummel was said to be so moved that he later improvised on the tune of *Der blinde Knabe* (D833) which he had just heard performed. Schubert was sufficiently impressed by the great man's interest that in the following year, 1828, he was to dedicate the final three piano sonatas to Hummel. It is ironic that Hummel, by the time of their publication in 1838, was already dead and that the publisher should decide as an alternative to confer the dedication on Robert Schumann, who formed a less than favourable opinion of the works.

Many commentators record a meeting in 1823 between Schubert and Carl Maria von Weber when on a visit to Vienna for the production of his new opera *Euryanthe*. Though Schubert's senior by 10 years, the famous composer and conductor had expressed his deep appreciation of Schubert's music. This led him, as related by Josef von Spaun, to ask for Schubert's opinion on *Euryanthe*. The opinion, as recalled, was that while the opera was of excellent workmanship, there was a conspicuous lack of melody which rendered it greatly inferior to *Der Freischütz*. The frankness of this judgement, unsurprisingly, is said to have resulted in the cessation of any further goodwill, although Weber should certainly have valued the advice.

COMPOSERS AFTER SCHUBERT'S TIME

A mere 20 months after Beethoven's death Schubert himself was dead, mourned by many friends and admirers, but attracting none of the public recognition of his great mentor or of his fellow composers. His music lay scattered, still mostly in manuscript copy, throughout Vienna and further afield. The task of collecting together and collating the compositions and of presenting Schubert's music to the world has been discussed earlier. And we have seen that it would be well over three decades, longer than Schubert's whole life span, before the world outside Vienna began to appreciate, with the aid of the first biography, the true extent and value of the music. There were, however, a small number of composers who played a part in the process of bringing Schubert's works to public notice.

The young Franz Liszt, as we have seen, was resident in Vienna in 1822 – 23 when, in addition to giving concerts as an 11-year-old prodigy, he took composition lessons with Salieri. During his time in Vienna, although the two composers are not recorded as having met, Liszt became aware of and admired Schubert's *lieder*. As a result, from 1833 onwards, Liszt began transcribing, performing and publishing his transcriptions of some 60 of the *lieder* plus other works. One is left wondering what influence the transcriptions had on Liszt's own subsequent compositions. Robert Schumann, a near contemporary of Liszt, had likewise become acquainted with Schubert's piano music and, through his visit to Vienna in 1838, became the go-between in securing the performance of the *Great* C Major Symphony in 1839.

There can be no doubt that Schumann's flowering as a composer of *lieder* owed much to his great predecessor, the beauty of whose works he revered but never surpassed. In the same context, Felix Mendelssohn was the enthusiastic recipient of the *Great* C Major Symphony and became an ardent admirer of those works of Schubert that were available up to his death in 1847. He was already a well-established composer by 1839 when he first saw Schubert's symphonies but must have been aware of his *lieder* which were in wide circulation during the 1830s. Were they an influence on his well-known *Lieder ohne Worte*? and was this an unspoken homage to the master of *lied*?

BRAHMS AND MAHLER

We then pass to a generation of composers who had no knowledge of the Vienna of Schubert's day, but who were influenced by his music as it emerged during the decades following the performance and publication of the *Great* C Major Symphony. Brahms, as a young man, had various connections with Schubert, including a teacher who had studied with Karl Maria von Bocklet, friend of Schubert and dedicatee of the Sonata D850. Brahms, as a celebrated pianist, had performed much of Schubert's piano music, had accompanied *Die schöne Müllerin* and had made his own (unpublished) transcriptions of many of the *lieder*. In 1863 on his first visit to Vienna, which was subsequently to become his home, he acquired a large amount of the piano music from the publisher Spina.

Some years later Brahms was invited to participate in the *Gesamtausgabe* project. He was initially resistant but finally became supportive and chaired the board of management. His editing of the piano compositions included restoring a section deleted by Schubert in the manuscript of the *Drei Klavierstücke* (D946). There is general recognition that Schubert was an important influence on Brahms' compositions, which can be seen through a number of works including the First String Sextet and the F Minor Piano Quintet. The Sextet was originally composed as a string quintet with two cellos; and the Piano Quintet, which shares various key relationships with Schubert's String Quintet, was originally composed as a two-cello quintet, in both cases an obvious tribute to Schubert. Brahms also made a study of the final B flat Piano Sonata (D960), his performance of which was recorded by Clara Schumann in her diary, notable at a time when the final sonatas were neither well known nor well regarded.

A decade after Brahms, Mahler studied the piano sonatas of Schubert along with those of Beethoven and Liszt; but the influence of Schubert clearly went further. While composing his Third Symphony he was also making an arrangement for string orchestra of the *Death and the Maiden* Quartet, of which the second movement, containing the song variations, was performed in Hamburg in 1894. In the Fourth Symphony, resemblances have been noted between the main theme of the first movement and the first movement of Schubert's E flat Sonata (D568); and between Mahler's song *Das himmlische Leben* and the finale of Schubert's D Major Sonata (D850). However, the deeper question is how far Mahler was influenced by Schubert's pioneering song cycles in his own works? Surely the early *Lieder eines fahrenden Gesellen* must acknowledge, as a major part of its inspiration, Schubert's *Winterreise*, with which it shares its hopeless love theme, even concluding with the young man lying down under a linden tree.

DVOŘÁK AND OTHERS

Antonin Dvořák, a contemporary of Brahms and Mahler, wrote in 1894* that while Schubert's fame had grown steadily, it would increase still further in the next century. Quoting Anton Rubinstein's opinion that Bach, Beethoven, and Schubert were 'the highest summits in music,' Dvořák added Mozart to the list, noting that Schubert and Mozart had much in common in their delicate sense of instrumental colouring, spontaneous and irrepressible flow of melody and instinctive command of the means of expression. Of Schubert's symphonies, Dvořák did not hesitate to place Schubert next to Beethoven. Citing the great German musicologist Dr Hugo Riemann, he considered that both Schumann and Liszt, in their use of harmony, were descendants of Schubert, and acknowledged his own great obligation to him. At a broader level, the free spirit that one senses in Dvořák's music is surely the manifestation of an outlook not based on classical rules but on the delight at the possibilities of creating music of original beauty. The two composers, separated

---

* *The Century*, New York, 1894.

by more than half a century, hailed from the same soil, figuratively, as well as geographically.

Other nineteenth-century composers who have acknowledged their debt to Schubert include Hector Berlioz and Anton Bruckner. Of twentieth-century composers, Richard Strauss, Anton Webern, Francis Poulenc, Heitor Villa-Lobos, George Crumb and Hans Zender have each paid homage to Schubert's influence on their works. But few have been more generous in their appreciation of Schubert and his influence on their music than Benjamin Britten. He regularly performed the *lieder* with his companion Peter Pears, as well as the piano duets. He marvelled at the works of the last period from *Winterreise* up to the String Quintet, which he referred to as the richest and most productive 18 months in musical history.

We have thus seen, in a rapid tour of European music in the nineteenth and twentieth centuries, how Schubert's influence was accepted and embraced by the leaders of musical thought and development. They had no need to await the gradual development of public appreciation. Once enough of Schubert's music had been published, its study became part of any composer's armoury, albeit some decades later than it should have been. And while later composers would build on Schubert's harmonic innovations, the *lieder* remained and remains a unique body of work never to be surpassed.

CHAPTER 19
NOTABLE SCHUBERTIANS

Schubert scholarship has from the outset attracted enthusiasts who, without exception, have been motivated by the beauty of the music and lured by the undiscovered gems to be found in it; and none have been disappointed or left unrewarded for their devoted work. They are referred to as the Schubertians. This chapter records some of the celebrated Schubertians of the past century and more, whose contributions to the spread of knowledge and appreciation of the music of Franz Schubert has been notable, and in some cases seminal.

The selection here presented includes the outstanding Viennese supporters of the nineteenth and early twentieth century and three notable English authorities, two of whom would be described as 'amateur' and just one a professional musicologist. These are followed by four performing musicians, two having originated from outside Britain, but all of whom have become major contributors to the musical life in this country.

NIKOLAUS DUMBA (1830–1900)

As a successful industrialist and politician, Nikolaus Dumba became a major philanthropist, funding many of the projects aimed at the promotion and celebration of the works of Franz Schubert. He was of Austrian and Greek parentage and amassed a great fortune, much of which he devoted to the arts in both Austria and Greece. In Vienna he was a major donor for the Musikverein building and the main funder of the Schubert monument in the Stadtpark, known as the Denkmal. As already seen, Dumba sought out and purchased a large collection of the Schubert manuscripts which he subsequently bequeathed to the Musikverein. He was also reputed to be a fine singer of the *lieder*.

When the Vienna Ringstrasse was being created in place of the outdated defensive walls, he acquired a prominent site on which to build a palatial mansion, opposite which was sited the Schubert memorial (largely funded by him). Among the treasures which adorned the mansion was the celebrated painting by Gustav Klimt of Schubert seated at the piano surrounded by ladies. The round ceiling of the main reception room was adorned with a painting by Friedrich Schilcher symbolically depicting different aspects of Schubert's works. Sadly the mansion together with the paintings was destroyed during the Second World War; but the section of the Ringstrasse on which the mansion was built has, since 1928, been re-named the Schubertring.

EUSEBIUS MANDYCZEWSKI (1857–1929)

A true descendant of the Austro-Hungarian Empire, Eusebius Mandyczewski was the son of an Orthodox priest from present-day Ukraine, his mother being from what is now Romania, both then part of the Empire. He studied in Vienna where he encountered Gustav Nottebohm, the compiler of one of the early catalogues of Schubert's works, as well as those by Johannes Brahms.

His marked musical abilities led to early ambitions as a composer. But once this was abandoned, he embarked on a career as teacher and conductor and became archivist of the Musikverein. Here he worked with Brahms and was a close associate of Nikolaus Dumba and regular visitor to his palatial residence on the Ring. He was a man of boundless energy and enthusiasm much of which he directed to the music of Franz Schubert. He was therefore ideally placed to contribute to the great *Gesamtausgabe* project for which he undertook the herculean task of editing the *lieder*.

When the work began in 1887 there were 480 songs published, with more than 200 further manuscripts to be collated and edited, these being located in different places. Fortunately, many were then in the possession of Nikolaus Dumba who had purchased large numbers of them whenever the opportunity arose. At the outset no-one appreciated the magnitude of the task and it was Mandyczewski who took the decision that the whole field must be covered by publishing all variants of every song, which should then be arranged in chronological order. The resulting collection occupied 10 volumes, which was finally welcomed by many who had initially opposed the scheme, including Brahms.

Mandyczewski also undertook editing of the masses and other sacred works, the male-voice part songs, quintets and string trios, with others contributing to the quartets and works for female and mixed chorus. Mandyczewski continued to promote Schubert's music into the 1920s and was one of the principal organisers of the Schubert centennial Congress staged in Vienna in November 1928. He died the following year having devoted his energies selflessly to the cause he loved.

OTTO ERICH DEUTSCH (1883–1967)

As the sole author of the now standard collection of documents pertaining to the life and works of Franz Schubert, Dr Otto Erich

Deutsch is rightly celebrated as the leading Schubertian of his or of any generation. His *Schubert Reader: A Life of Franz Schubert in Letters and Documents* was published in 1946, in England and in English, after an early German edition had been published in 1914. Deutsch followed the *Schubert Reader* with his *Schubert Thematic Catalogue* of 1951 in which, for the first time, he assigned Deutsch or 'D' numbers to the whole of Schubert's output. This was followed by a volume of collected *Memoirs by his Friends* in 1957, published in German and translated into English in 1958.

His scholarship thus extended for more than half a century and also included major studies of Handel and Mozart. Originally a native of Vienna, his work spanned two world wars, the second resulting in his move to England to escape Nazi persecution. At the outbreak of war in 1939 he was interned on the Isle of Man where he had the opportunity to mix with other German Jewish refugees, including the members of the future Amadeus Quartet. He was eventually allowed to settle in Cambridge where he was able to resume his scholarship with the second and enlarged edition of the *Documents*, now in English. At the outset of his work on Schubert, Deutsch took the decision, instead of writing the definitive biography himself, to devote his energies to collecting and collating all the extant documents relevant to Schubert's life and music. He started with the correspondence from and to Schubert himself, then moved on to correspondence between others concerning events in Schubert's life, and extended this to diary entries, press notices and any other contemporary written or printed material capable of throwing light on Schubert's life and times. He thus denied himself the satisfaction of composing the biography, and selflessly left it to others to use his scholarship and efforts in composing biographical works with the use of the *Documents*. As he commented in the Preface: 'ever since 1914 it has been difficult, not so much to write a Schubert biography, but to refrain from writing one.' Deutsch was not the first Schubertian, nor the first to catalogue the works, but he had the satisfaction of adding his name to the later catalogue of works so that Deutsch is constantly on the mind of those enjoying Schubert's works.

Being a native of Schubert's own city, Deutsch was able, before the First World War, to visit virtually every place in which Schubert had lived and worked, and at a time when there had been no major changes to much of the city. He was also able to correspond with, and meet relatives of, those who had more direct knowledge of Schubert's life, and thus to research and assemble the documentary records before any were lost or destroyed. When publishing the first edition of the *Documents* in 1914 he always intended it to be supplemented by further research. In the event, this was completed in Cambridge where Eric Blom, as translator, proposed its publication in English. Thus the English edition, greatly enlarged compared to the original German edition, was republished in German only in 1964. In 1949 he met Maurice Brown, a much younger English Schubert enthusiast, with whom he established a close and lasting relationship, largely by post.* Dr Deutsch returned to Vienna in 1951 where he died in 1967. His reputation remains as the greatest of Schubert scholars.

MAURICE BROWN (1906–1975)

From a generation after Deutsch, Maurice J. E. Brown made his career as a teacher, becoming the head of science at Marlborough Grammar School. At the age of 15 he encountered the *Unfinished* Symphony and began what was to be a lifelong study of the works of Franz Schubert.

---

* See *Dear Brown*: an account of the exchanges between Deutsch and Brown between 1949 and 1967 by Paul Reid, published by the Schubert Institute Research Centre.

Maurice J. E. Brown

In the course of his studies he gained a music degree and befriended Eric Blom and Otto Erich Deutsch, both of whom he venerated. His mastery of the German language allowed him to assist in the translation of Deutsch's work and the two men established a close relationship during the remainder of Deutsch's life. While continuing his main teaching career, Brown contributed articles on Schubert to the musical journals, and in 1954 published his first book, *Schubert's Variations*. This was followed in 1958 by *Schubert: A Critical Biography* and in 1966 by *Essays on Schubert*. He also wrote the Schubert section for the *Grove Dictionary of Music and Musicians* and continued as editor to the 1980 edition.

Maurice Brown became the leading English authority on the works of Schubert and broadcast frequently on Schubert's music. His *Essays on Schubert* cover a wide range of current topics including studies of lately discovered drafts of well-known works with which he was able, finally, to disprove the notion that Schubert composed straight into final copy with no preliminary sketches. In doing so he also debunked the popular notion, even entertained by George Grove, that Schubert must have been in receipt of divine inspiration. The essays also cover the problematic piano sonatas of which a substantial portion are unfinished and undated, the much overlooked genres of male voice part songs (once the rage in Vienna), and the dance music (also highly popular in Schubert's lifetime).

At an early stage in his studies Brown reportedly decided to devote his life to research and writing on Schubert and his works, the fruits of which still adorn our bookshelves. In the course of his contacts with other scholars he amassed a great collection of documents and correspondence all of which are now housed in the Brotherton Library in the University of Leeds.

JOHN REED (1909–1999)

Like his near contemporary Maurice Brown, John Reed was from a distinguished line of English enthusiasts who enjoyed a second career as a Schubert scholar after his retirement. He studied English at London University and began his professional life as an English teacher. After war service he joined the BBC where he worked in the education department as producer and administrator until his retirement. His work on Schubert began with an article in 1959 on the so-called Gastein Symphony. By the 1960s it was increasingly accepted that the *Great* C Major Symphony was probably composed in 1825 and not 1828. But in 1972 Reed's reputation was established by his first book, *Schubert: The Final Years*, in which he authoritatively demonstrated that the Gastein Symphony was indeed composed in 1825 and was one and the same as the *Great* C Major Symphony. Reed's publications continued with his *Schubert Song Companion* of 1985 which was, remarkably, the first book to discuss each of Schubert's solo songs.

John Reed

Reed generously shared his research through his publications and through assistance to other scholars including Maurice Brown. He was instrumental in founding the Schubert Institute (UK) in 1991 and became its first chairman, steering it to become a leading forum for the discussion and performance of Schubert's works. In 1997 he organised the inauguration of the Schubert Institute Research Centre within the University of Leeds. John Reed also became honorary director of the Manchester Camerata orchestra and was awarded honorary membership of Vienna's International Franz Schubert Institute.

BRIAN NEWBOULD (B. 1936)

After studies at the University of Bristol, Brian Newbould decided to channel his musical talents into an academic career. In the course of teaching harmony at a number of universities and developing an increasing appreciation of Schubert's music, he was invited to write a completion of Symphony No 7 and subsequently of the *Unfinished* Symphony. This experience drew him yet further into the fascinating challenge of the many and varied unfinished compositions left by Schubert, and led to an increasing interest in the techniques of completing the uncompleted. His academic career eventually led to a chair as professor at Hull University, now Emeritus, where he has been able to develop his unique facility for absorbing and assuming the role of the composer. His work has led, over several decades, to achieving the completion of a large number of Schubert's otherwise unfinished works, all of which have now been recorded, many having been broadcast extensively.

Professor Brian Newbould

Brian Newbould is the author of many books on Schubert's works, the latest being his *Schubert's Workshop*, in which he presents a full analysis of the many facets of Schubert's approach to harmony. For some years he has also presented, in many different countries, lectures and introductions to his completions of Schubert's unfinished works. These now include, in addition to Schubert's Symphonies No 7 and No 8, the cryptic and rough sketch found after Schubert's death and now referred to as Symphony No 10. He has also prepared performing versions of the incomplete symphonic fragments D615 (1818) and D708a (1820). Other unfinished works for which he has created completions include the *Quartettsatz* and the *Reliquie* Piano Sonata. In addition to completions, he has adapted a suite from the early opera *Die Zauberharfe* (*The Magic Harp*), which was given its world premiere and subsequently recorded in Vienna in 2019. It was in the course of studying the score of this opera that he discovered Schubert's use of the palindrome – the repetition of a section of the score written out backwards. This musical device, which appeared in the music of J. S. Bach and Haydn but was unknown during the nineteenth century, was described by Brian as a secret shared with the composer himself!

DIETRICH FISCHER-DIESKAU (1925–2012)

The German baritone Dietrich Fischer-Dieskau became, certainly in England, the best-known post-war Schubert interpreter who recorded a very large number of the *lieder* including the song cycles several times over. Drafted into the German Army during the Second World War, he was taken prisoner in Italy and in this capacity spent two years in England before returning to complete his studies. His debut was in Freiburg in 1947 and thereafter he performed throughout Europe, particularly in London where he became the leading interpreter of the *lieder*. Notable recordings of *Die schöne Müllerin* and *Schwanengesang* were made at London Abbey Road studios in October 1951 with Gerald Moore. His output of recordings has been immense and includes eight recordings of *Winterreise*, his final recording being with Alfred Brendel.

The recordings represent an apparently insatiable desire to achieve perfection. His repertoire extended far beyond Schubert and beyond *lieder*, to include the operas of Strauss and Wagner, as well as the oratorios of J. S. Bach. In 1962 he sang in the first performance of Britten's *War Requiem* in Coventry Cathedral. He inspired a generation of new post-war *lieder* singers in Britain and elsewhere and, in doing so, created a new audience for *lieder* recitals, particularly of Schubert and especially in London.

GERALD MOORE (1899–1987)

Born in England, Gerald Moore's family emigrated, before the First World War, to Canada where he studied, but he returned to London after the war and continued at The Guildhall School of Music and Drama. Intending to make a career as a concert pianist he discovered a penchant for accompanying, particularly singers. This led to his debut in 1921 playing with soloists, after which he became established as a regular accompanist for HMV, recording many of the Schubert *lieder* with celebrated artists including Elisabeth Schwarzkopf and, later, Dietrich Fischer-Dieskau. During the middle years of the twentieth century, he was the best-known *lieder* pianist, frequently touring in Europe but with regular appearances in London.

Moore created a tradition of *lieder* accompanists and is said to have played for every eminent solo singer and instrumentalist who came to perform in London. He elevated the art of accompaniment to the level of an equal partner, contributing a sensitivity and remarkable sense of rhythm. He retired from public performances in 1967 but continued recording until 1975. At his farewell concert in London he accompanied Victoria de los Angeles, Elisabeth Schwarzkopf and Dietrich Fischer-Dieskau. The concert concluded with an arrangement for solo piano of Schubert's *An die Musik*. His book, *The Unashamed Accompanist*, written in 1943, was subsequently translated into German, for which Fischer-Dieskau wrote in his introduction: 'There is no more of that pale shadow at the keyboard: he is always an equal with his partner.'

ALFRED BRENDEL (1931–2025)

Born in what was then Czechoslovakia in the years leading up to the Second World War, and into a family with no notable musical tradition, Alfred Brendel, after showing early and obvious musical ability, studied the piano initially at the Graz Conservatory, Austria. However, it was wartime and at the age of 14 he was sent to Yugoslavia to dig trenches to resist the advance of the Russian Army. He survived the war and was able to continue his studies. Despite receiving no more formal lessons beyond the age of 16, he gave recitals from the age of 17, which led to awards in international competitions and to recordings, the first of which was made in 1950.

He progressively built a reputation for performing and recording the works of Beethoven, Liszt, Brahms, Mozart and especially Schubert. He seldom performed Chopin, despite regarding his music as 'the most glorious achievement in piano music, after Beethoven and Schubert.' During the 1970s he toured extensively, and achieved a major following in London where he decided to take up permanent residence. He continued to live in Hampstead during his retirement but died on 17th June 2025, aged 94. His many recordings will remain a monument to his achievements and his artistry. Alfred Brendel was president of the Schubert Institute (UK).

GRAHAM JOHNSON (B. 1950)

Born in what was then Southern Rhodesia, he moved to London to continue studies at the Royal Academy of Music (RAM). From early in his career he was inspired by the recitals of Peter Pears and Benjamin Britten, which drew his career towards accompanying rather than performing as a soloist. Thus, after graduating from the RAM, he continued studies with Gerald Moore and Geoffrey Parsons. He became the official pianist at Peter Pears' first masterclasses at the Snape Maltings, which brought him into contact with Benjamin Britten. In 1976, he formed The Songmakers' Almanac to explore neglected areas of piano-accompanied vocal music, along with other notable performers including Felicity Lott, Ann Murray, Richard Jackson and Anthony Rolfe Johnson.

He is particularly noted for his recordings of *lieder*, which culminated in the Hyperion series of 37 CDs containing the complete *lieder* of Franz Schubert issued in 2005 with three supplementary CDs of *lieder* by contemporaries and friends of Schubert. He was the accompanist for the complete series. He has also devised many programmes of *lieder* and has written notes for *The Complete Songs* of Robert Schumann, Johannes Brahms and other composers. He has recorded for other labels including EMI Classics and Deutsche Grammophon. He is the author of many books, including the 3-volume *Franz Schubert, the Complete Songs* (Yale) and *The Songmakers' Almanac: Twenty Years of Recitals in London*. Graham Johnson is Professor of Accompaniment at the Guildhall School of Music and Drama and has led many song festivals.

THE OTHER SCHUBERTIANS

There are, naturally, many other deserving individuals, from the nineteenth to the twenty-first century, who have made significant contributions to Schubert scholarship and the advancement of our knowledge and appreciation of the composer. Many are mentioned in these pages, but there will always be a greater and unsung company of persons who appreciate the unique qualities of Schubert's music, whether actively or simply as listeners. They are all Schubertians.

CHAPTER 20
HAS THE REAL SCHUBERT YET EMERGED?

More recent writings on the life of Franz Schubert* simply pass over the habitual myths which became attached to his life and character over much of the two centuries that have elapsed since his day. But it is still instructive to recall those myths and consider how they ever arose; which was through a combination of ignorance, such as the notion that his manuscripts bore no signs of either preparation or of correction, or simple malice, such as claims that he was socially inept, lazy and often drunk. None of those notions begin to explain how works of such beauty could be created by such a person – and hence the further myth that Schubert must have been a somnambulist, in receipt of divine dictation (a belief entertained even by Johann Michael Vogl, the man who saw the products of the supposed dictation at first hand). The myths perhaps begin to explain the heartless way in which Schubert was virtually dropped and abandoned by the Viennese concert-going public from his death, with the few notable exceptions of brother Ferdinand and a small circle of friends, and Johann

---

* Particularly the biography by Elizabeth Norman McKay and *A Musical Wayfarer*, by Lorraine Byrne Bodley.

Michael Vogl who, whatever his personal thoughts, continued to sing Schubert's *lieder* up to his own death.

It is evident that Schubert must have worked at an incredible level of concentration to produce the volume of work he created, of which casual critics and even close friends were simply unaware. But this still begs the question, who was the real Schubert? And, after stripping away the myths, what can we know of him? Should we conclude that the amazing level of work he devoted to his compositions left him with little time for normal socialising and led to his documented failures to attend social appointments, even musical ones? The evidence is quite the reverse. He is known to have taken lengthy breaks for walking tours and to have attended social and especially musical events. However, when composing we can conclude that his attention was fully committed to the exclusion of outside distractions, especially social ones. The huge volume of compositions left to us was the result of his legendary fluency and speed of composing, testified to by many contemporaries, together with a degree of application and concentration that few will ever experience.

But apart from his output, which is unchallengeable, there is still a paucity of evidence throwing light on the real Schubert, even in the great volume of material assembled by the likes of Luib, von Hellborn, and latterly Otto Erich Deutsch. For despite its volume, the material tells us little that can be relied on about the man himself. Many of his friends and acquaintances wrote detailed accounts of Schubert's life and character, both after his death and subsequently some 30 years later when approached to assist in a projected biography. But these accounts still tell us very little about Schubert the man. And Maurice Brown devotes a whole section of his *Critical Biography** to laying bare the deliberate and usually self-serving fabrications committed under the guise of affectionate recollection. Most of the popular anecdotes

---

* *Schubert, a Critical Biography*, Chapter IX part V.

about Schubert's lifestyle date from the later reminiscences and were simply made up or had little or no foundation.

RECOLLECTIONS OF SPAUN

Whose recollection can one trust? The person universally regarded by the Schubert circle as his true friend and the 'best and noblest'* of them was, without doubt, Josef von Spaun. Schubert dedicated a number of works to him and owed much to his support in the early days at the Stadtkonvikt, and in later years as an enthusiastic host of Schubertiads. He was the man who attempted, without result, to attract the attention of Johann Wolfgang von Goethe to Schubert's settings of 16 of his poems. Spaun was a regular correspondent with Schubert and had returned to Vienna in 1826 from a government posting in Lemberg, which had furnished him with the means to set up a large residence in which to host musical parties. From this point he saw a great deal of Schubert in the crucial final two years of his life, seeing him for the last time just days before his death. Spaun wrote a lengthy obituary in the months after the death,† which was edited and published in March and April 1829. Thereafter he wrote three further extensive notes: the first in 1858 in response to requests for biographical information from Luib; the second in 1864; and a further note in the same year correcting information which had then appeared in the von Hellborn biography.

From these sources, which remained consistent despite the passage of 30 years or more, we can get what is the most reliable picture of the composer as observed by a true friend. Thus we can learn that, while still a schoolboy, after being taken for the first time to hear operas by Weigl and Gluck 'he was moved to his depths and to tears;' and this experience was followed by the

---

* Per Moritz von Schwind.
† Deutsch, *Docs* p 865-879.

keenest study of all Gluck's scores. Schubert, unsurprisingly, had a phenomenal memory which retained works, once heard, in detail. As to his extraordinary rapidity in composition, Spaun comments that the lavish stream of melodies 'seemed only to grow by its outpouring.' In his more mature years Schubert was not constrained by the conventions of society and could offend by his ruthless frankness. His work as a composer was closely regulated with 9am to 2pm devoted to composition or study, but the rest of the day was devoted to family or friends, often with long excursions into the Viennese countryside. Aware of the popular notion (shared by Vogl) that Schubert produced his finest music by inspiration without any conscious activity of his own, the idea was surely dispelled by Schubert's enthusiastic discussions about his compositions with friends. While he was reputed to lack social graces, to his close and now distinguished friend von Spaun, he was 'uncommonly sincere, open, friendly, modest, grateful, sociable, communicative in joy and reserved in sorrow, yet free from all bitterness.'

ANOTHER SIDE OF HIS CHARACTER

Yet he was also human, and the reluctance of friends to touch on socially unacceptable failings is understandable. A man whose life was shortened by syphilis had not lived a strictly moral life in the understanding of the time. But there was nothing unusual, particularly in artistic circles in the nineteenth century, with contracting the disease: a catalogue of celebrated artists who suffered the same fate can readily be compiled, starting with his great admirer, Robert Schumann, and also Hugo Wolf. In Schubert's case the details of his social life, which may be seen as conducive to his having contracted the disease, have been the subject of much speculative writing in the last three decades. These include suggestions of homosexuality* among the Schu-

---

* Maynard Solomon: 'Franz Schubert and the Peacocks of Benvenuto Cellini,' 'circle' and exotic practices inspired and led by close friend and collaborator Franz von Schober.

The debate has more recently been renewed,* this time centred on Robert Schumann's seemingly casual use of the term *Mädchencharakter*, which is interpreted as indicative of womanliness or femininity, especially compared to the supposed 'masculinity' of the likes of Ludwig van Beethoven. To this 'evidence' might be added the very real observations made upon the disinterring of the bodies of both Schubert and Beethoven in 1863 when Schubert's skull was reported as showing a 'delicate almost womanly organisation.'† None of this, however, is of any account. It can have no relevance whatever to the music he created, nor should it affect the picture of Schubert conveyed so far, of a sincere, open and sociable genius who was consumed by the great music he surely knew that he was creating. In any event Schubert left us with a death mask which reveals strong masculine features, revealing anything but 'delicate almost womanly' features, as pointed out by Alfred Brendel.‡

Perhaps the issue can be resolved by recalling the context in which Schumann coined his somewhat strange description, when discussing the Sonata in C for four hands, D812, of 1824:

> To one who has some degree of cultivation and feeling, Beethoven and Schubert may be recognised, yet held apart, on their very first pages. Schubert is a maidenly character [*Mädchencharakter*] compared to the other, far more talkative, softer, broader; compared to him he is a child, sporting carelessly among the giants. Such is the relation these symphonic movements bear to those of Beethoven, and, in their inwardness, they could not have been imagined by any other than Schubert.

19th-Century Music 27 August 1989 Vol 12, No 3 (Spring, 1989), pp 193-206; Donald Henehan: 'The Dark Side of Schubert,' *New York Times*.

* Scott Messing: *Schubert in the European Imagination*, 2007, 2 vols.
† Quoted in von Hellborn Chapter XVII.
‡ See *Alfred Brendel on Music*, p 152.

SELF-AWARENESS

How does one assess or describe the personality of an individual who must be aware of his own artistic greatness? Schubert was reportedly embarrassed by the enthusiastic reception of his work and was content for the performer to receive the praise of the audience, while he sat, characteristically, at the piano out of the limelight. What did he think about his own compositions? We know that shortly after composing the four great final works, the String Quintet and the three piano sonatas, he engaged in correspondence with publishers about the E flat Trio, almost casually mentioning these great works along with 'several songs by Heine of Hamburg.'* His concern had switched to the mundane needs of publishing and getting paid. Perhaps one should conclude that he had no time to dwell on the world's ingratitude and indifference, content to know that he had created works of which the world would eventually realise the greatness.

It is related that, on one occasion, he spent an evening out with friends Franz Lachner and Eduard von Bauernfeld to try out the new vintage. It was an evening which ended in a hostelry in the Vienna suburbs where, as reported, Schubert lost his temper with a group of musicians who greeted the famous composer with a request to write something for them. This seemed to touch a nerve, as perhaps emphasising the world's seeming indifference. He is reported as having exploded with the words:

> I am Schubert – Franz Schubert whom everybody knows and recognises! who has written great things and beautiful things, that you don't begin to understand ... I am Schubert, Franz Schubert! And don't you forget it.†

---

* Deutsch: 'Letter 2 October 1828 to Probst,' *Docs* No 1152.
† Deutsch: 'Memoir (3) of Eduard von Bauernfeld,' *Schubert: Memoirs by his Friends*, p 231.

The *Memoir* was written in 1869 and, given the circumstances, is unlikely to represent more than what the writer thought – more than 40 years after the event – could have happened, given the celebrity that Schubert had acquired in following years. However, such an outburst was not inconsistent with the character which emerges from other historical notes; and could be seen as reflective of some of the more dramatic episodes injected into his music, such as the Andantino of the Piano Sonata D959. But by 1828 he was past any verbal protest and was content to let the world take its course which, fortunately for us, was the right course in the end.

MUSICAL FORMS

In assessing Schubert's music there is no avoiding the constant holding up of Beethoven as the role model which he is said to have striven to emulate but always fell just short of equalling. While it is universally accepted that Schubert's *lieder* outshone anything that went before, and in the view of many, anything that followed too, his musical achievements are still judged alongside Beethoven's treatment of musical forms, in comparison to which Schubert, it is said, cannot rival his great contemporary. Many examples can be cited, from his symphonies to his piano sonatas, including the last six composed, where Schubert simply diverged from the Beethoven model resulting, in the eyes of earlier critics, in works which could not be seen as conforming to the expected model. The critic Anthony Hopkins[*] once characterised Schubert's symphonies, in comparison to Beethoven's towering structures, as works still 'wandering in the foothills.' Such was the general view throughout the nineteenth and much of the twentieth century of the first six symphonies, even after they had been rescued by Grove and Sullivan in 1867 and performed to universal appreciation at the Crystal Palace. This

---

[*] BBC: *Talking about Music* C 1962.

criticism extended even to the mature works including the last two symphonies. As Mosco Carner wrote:

> 'There is no inner development or growth that inevitably leads to a last climax in the finale. Different facets of the idea are shown, yet the idea itself is not elaborated or put through a dialectic form of argument and counter argument.'*

The role model demonstrating that which Schubert lacked was, of course, Beethoven. But now a new order of criticism and analysis has taken over which no longer regards Beethoven's treatment of musical form as the only way, and sees Schubert's approach as not only original but the natural outcome of his unique artistry. To illustrate what is meant here, readers will appreciate that much of the output of composers of the late eighteenth and into the nineteenth century was written in so-called sonata form. In classical terms, this denotes music having a first subject or group of themes which may be developed but is expected to lead on to a second contrasting subject or themes, conventionally in the dominant key to the opening – that is, if the work begins in B flat, the second subject should be in F. This is the 'exposition' which is usually followed by a development section, after which the subjects are repeated but traditionally all in the home key, in which the movement should also end. While Beethoven used sonata form in many different ways, his treatment of the development section is seen as demonstrating how subjects and themes may be elaborated and 'put through a dialectic form of argument and counter argument.[†] Beethoven's approach is to take the elements of the themes presented and then reveal all their musical potential.

Schubert, while being fully aware of Beethoven's lead, took his own course from his earliest works in the form. Nothing

---

* Mosco Carner: *Schubert: A Symposium*, ed Gerald Abraham, 1946, p 26.
† *Ibid.*

could illustrate Schubert's approach to musical form better than the first movement of his final Piano Sonata in B flat (D960) which is universally regarded as a work of unsurpassed beauty. But in Beethoven's terms, Schubert's approach gives rise to the faults and aberrations which traditionalists and critics have found objectionable, and may have been the cause of the work being brushed aside by Schumann and ignored by musicologists for a century.

AN OPENING MOVEMENT

The B flat Sonata begins with a striking (some would say ethereal) hymn-like theme which, like many of Schubert's themes, is one of great and memorable beauty; it has the inherent quality of being easily recognisable when appearing in different guises later in the movement. The first statement of the theme leads, after a mysterious bass trill and repeat, to it reappearing but now in the remote key of F sharp and subtly modified, starting not on the tonic note but still on B flat, which is now the third note of the scale. The music works up to the first crescendo with a dramatic key shift back to B flat and then to a second subject, consisting characteristically of two themes played together, one a falling dotted theme which will be heard in different forms as the movement progresses. But the second subject is not in the conventional key of F but again in F sharp, the key in which we earlier heard the opening theme but now Schubert uses F sharp Minor, which then moderates through D Minor, C Major and B flat, ending the exposition in the expected key of F. The development proceeds immediately, after an abrupt key change in just three chords, to the remote key of C sharp Minor (the key of the second movement and the dominant key of F sharp), in which we hear a further but easily recognisable version of the opening melody. This leads to an *arpeggio* figure passing through the keys of A Major and B Major and finally moderating back to B flat for a dramatic section with triplets in the right hand set against dual time in the left. Then a disarmingly simple *arpeggio* figure reveals the return of the first theme, *pianissimo* but in the remote key of D Minor, the mystery heightened by bass trills, which lead to the recapitulation. The first theme is heard in B flat and then in F sharp but this time modulating to A Major with the second pair of subjects heard in B Minor which modulates back to B flat for the final reprise of themes.

Thus laid out, the work sounds bewildering and one might wonder why the composer chooses a succession of keys through which to guide the music. But Schubert's sound world is soon perceived as modulating between the home keys of B flat and F and a series of remote keys that present an ever-changing but hauntingly beautiful and then inevitable progression of harmonies. While the opening theme appears in several different forms it is always recognisable as such, and there is no thought that it should be broken into fragments to be 'developed' as other composers might. The music is complete and the journey it undergoes fully justified in both aesthetic and classical terms. Schubert never composed without creating melodies which remain in the mind; and this movement abounds in them. The mysterious bass trill, heard in the opening, reappears in different places including the start of the recapitulation. Much could be written about the notes of F followed by a trill on F sharp, which may reveal something of the composer's intentions. It is a warning of the modulations to follow, and of the shift from the expected key of F, as the dominant key, to F sharp, a modulation used in other related works including the great String Quintet, which was most likely composed simultaneously with the sonata. The modulations, here and elsewhere, give the work an appearance of floating free of any fixed tonality.

The work could not have been written by Beethoven, nor especially could that master have composed the haunting theme that underpins the movement. It is pure Schubert and any comparison with external rules or standards is simply irrelevant and of no consequence. By general consent the works of Schubert's last months were the final flowering of his genius even though, in the case of the last sonatas, this has taken over a century for audiences to discover. Schubert's choice and presentation of musical forms is not a matter for comparative criticism but of analysis and admiration.

FINISHING THE UNFINISHED

Schubert left more unfinished works than any other major composer. Apart from the *Unfinished* Symphony, which might seem to owe something of its appeal to the very fact of being incomplete, there are a large number of piano compositions, *lieder* and many larger works including operas and two further symphonies that were left unfinished. This gives rise to two separate questions: first should any and if so which of the uncompleted works be completed? And secondly, how should the 'completions' be carried out? The first is a question anyone can hold an opinion on; the second is for the specialist musicologist and composer. A third question, which may provide the answer to the first, is why did Schubert leave works unfinished? The third question is addressed first.

The popular view about the unfinished works is that Schubert composed at such a fast pace, testified to by both observers and by dates and times inscribed on manuscripts, that if his inspiration momentarily failed, his fertile mind would come up with a new idea and a new work which displaced the one left unfinished. That may indeed explain some of the incomplete manuscripts. However, there are many manuscripts of *lieder* in which the first ideas for the poem were dropped and a second or even third attempt made to achieve the setting satisfactory to the composer. In some cases we are left with alternative complete settings of the same poem, but in others an incomplete manuscript was left. This, of course, tells us that some at least of the incomplete works were laid aside in favour of other ideas which, in the case of a piano work, would be a different composition. The detailed study of sketches also reveals how Schubert revised his first drafts. This has shown us, in a number of major works including the E flat Piano Trio (D929), how Schubert modified his first ideas to achieve the great work which we know today.*

This approach leads to the conclusion that some, at least, of the unfinished works were intentionally left because the composer could not see how the draft could be completed to his satisfaction. This fate is said to apply to the partly drafted Scherzo of the *Unfinished* Symphony itself, which has not deterred attempts to continue and complete the movement. But it remains a topic for debate whether and which of the unfinished works merit completion. At the very least it allows the music written down by Schubert to be heard, and avoids the shock of an abrupt ending if performed as left by the composer. Thus to revert to the first question posed, while any enthusiast may hold a view on whether works left unfinished should be completed, that view may be informed by detailed study of the works themselves.

As to the second question – how an unfinished work should be completed? – the objective must be to compose, as far as possible, what Schubert would have written had he decided to complete the work. The specialist composers who have undertaken this task will usually provide a detailed account of the decisions taken, of the related and completed works that have been studied to provide guidance, and of the analysis of the work as left by the composer to reveal its form and structure. Fortunately, for completions carried out in recent years, the composer/completer has invariably provided a detailed note with the CD made of the performance,† as well as publishing papers in the academic journals.

---

* M. Brown: 'Drafting the Masterpiece,' *Essays on Schubert*.
† See for example Brian Newbould's completion of the *Reliquie* Sonata D840 issued by Toccata Classics.

There are, however, other possible approaches. Where a work has been left with a whole movement uncomposed, there remains the possibility that the composer did compose the movement but decided to use it elsewhere. This is the case with the finale of the *Unfinished* Symphony where, on the basis of the key of the work (B Minor) and the timing of its composition, it has been proposed that the finale should be the B Minor first *entr'acte* of the incidental music to *Rosamunde*, composed only months after the first movements of the symphony and employing the same orchestral forces.* A different approach is needed where Schubert left only sketches. The possible solutions in the case of the Tenth Symphony, for which only fragments were written down in the last weeks of the composer's life, have already been discussed.

However, as computing techniques and particularly Artificial Intelligence (AI) continue to expand and to rival human thought processes, a different solution may be approaching, namely the use of AI to generate completions of uncompleted works. There can be little doubt that such an eventuality is possible and that computer-generated completions will become available. A different question will then arise, namely what to do with them? If they are to be taken seriously, it will be necessary for performers to study the resulting scores and to perform and record the newly generated works. In the case of orchestral works this will require orchestras and players together with a conductor to devote the time and resources necessary for a performance. It is evident that there will be many practical issues which may inhibit the development of AI-generated completions and impose limitations that cannot be foreseen at the present. But there will always remain the option for any audience of adhering to what Schubert wrote down and not proceeding beyond that.

---

* Brian Newbould: *Schubert's Workshop*, section 37, Routledge 2023.

ARRANGEMENTS AND ORCHESTRATIONS

A further issue which should be included is the editing and arranging of Schubert's music, usually with the objective of making it more accessible to the musical public. It can be argued that such a process is excusable since Schubert himself (in common with many earlier composers) recycled works as needed; for example the reuse of the overture to *Die Zauberharfe* for the incidental music to *Rosamunde*. And while there was no shortage of good tunes in Schubert's music, he clearly liked to make the most of a favourite melody, such as the *Rosamunde Entr'acte* or such favourite *lieder* as *Die Forelle* and *Trockne Blumen*. So the rearrangement of his music should not cause alarm. Still popular examples are Liszt transcriptions; as are the selection of Schubertian favourites used in the 1916 musical production, subsequently renamed in England as *Lilac Time*, already discussed. If such measures make the public more appreciative of Schubert's music the process should surely be applauded.

A different trend, which has an impeccable pedigree, is the orchestration of works written, typically for piano duet or simply as piano-accompanied *lieder*. Notable among these is the arrangement by Joseph Joachim, at the suggestion of Brahms who thought the work to be a lost symphony, of the celebrated Grand Duo in C (D812), in 1855. There have been a number of transcriptions of the famous F Minor Fantasia (D940), orchestrated by Felix Mottl in 1897, and many more of the smaller four-hand works and solo piano pieces. The orchestration of *lieder*, apart from the work of Liszt, was taken up by Berlioz with his orchestration of *Erlkönig*, in company with other celebrated composers including Offenbach and Brahms himself. And by the end of the nineteenth century with the advent of the gramophone, many of the earlier recordings with well-known *lieder* singers were given with anonymous orchestral accompaniment. Only later in the twentieth century did the practice give way to the purer approach to performing the music as written. But many of the more celebrated transcriptions remain in the repertoire and continue to spread the fame denied to the composer in his lifetime.

HAVE WE YET GOT THE BALANCE RIGHT?

The enormous and growing popularity of Schubert's music suggests that we might with advantage reconsider our current view of the composer, whose output is selectively offered to the public by both performers and concert promoters. Is there too much emphasis on the 'popular' works such as the final sonatas, the song cycles and half-a-dozen chamber works, and should we be paying off the debt of two centuries in which a large part of his output was ignored? Should we pay more regard to what Schubert considered important – his operas and church music and the many vocal works which are rarely if ever heard? Fortunately, while the concert halls will continue to be filled by performances of the song cycles, late sonatas and chamber works, more and more festivals are taking the opportunity to explore the less frequented repertoire.

The future, in the UK and throughout Europe and the USA, looks bright with the promise that the whole repertoire, as Schubert would have intended, can be placed before the discerning musical public to enjoy to the full. And of course in the new digital age there is no work of the master, however obscure, which is not now readily available at the touch of a screen or keyboard, thus facilitating direct interaction between the dead composer and his audience of two centuries further on.

CHAPTER 21
CONCLUSION

It is fashionable to explain Schubert's premature death as being of little significance, since he had lived a fuller life and composed more music than any other composer, however long-lived. Britten regarded the miraculous final year as a time in which Schubert composed the works he needed to compose, presumably to round off his life in a satisfactory way. But that is not the way Schubert saw it. His actions and words in the last weeks give no hint of impending death and certainly not of resignation or submission to an inevitable fate. Having written the final sonatas and the quintet, he set about sketching a new symphony and hatched the eternally enigmatic plan to take lessons in counterpoint. Without entering into a debate about why he should have thought lessons in counterpoint would be of any interest, he was, in the clearest terms, looking forward to the continuation of the life he had built for himself, as a composer of growing reputation whose genius would, one day, inevitably be recognised by the world.

SCHUBERT AT 80

So with respect to all those who would overlook the premature death as being less than the tragedy that it was, it is in order and still relevant to ask what Schubert might have achieved had he lived another five, 10 or 50 years. Where would the music of the nineteenth century have progressed had Schubert lived and continued to compose? And related to that question, what music would Schubert have composed had he lived another 50 years so that in the year 1878 he had passed the age of 80? It is worth noting that in that year Verdi attained the age of 64, lived on to compose his last opera in 1892 aged 78 and died at the age of 88.

From the early 1890s Mahler was composing symphonies infused with song, including both solo singers and choirs of increasing size. There could surely be no doubt that Schubert, with Beethoven's lead already in his mind, would soon have begun to explore the combination of choral and orchestral compositions, and that his bursting inspiration would have led to a new range of symphonies which would have anticipated Mahler by many decades. Indeed, his future compositions would certainly also have continued his development of new harmonic ideas. As Dvořák observed, citing the opinion of Dr Hugo Riemann, had Schubert lived another 30 years, he would have anticipated nearly everything that is original in the harmonies of Chopin, Wagner, Liszt, and Grieg.

But the field in which Schubert would certainly have excelled and become a leader of musical development is opera. The experience which Schubert never secured in his short lifetime was to study and learn from the demands imposed by stage productions of his operas, and to modify his compositions to fit the flow of the drama and the needs of staging and performing the works. It also goes without saying that he would, as his operatic composing developed, have secured the services of more worthy librettists and have learned to choose his subjects more wisely. No doubt this would have led him to consider other sources than the German poets and playwrights, particularly Shakespeare. One can only imagine the pleasure of attending a production, in German, of *Macbeth* or *Othello* by Franz Schubert.

FUTURE SCHOLARSHIP

The fad for speculating on Schubert's sexual proclivities is a prime example of wasted endeavour which leads nowhere. Indeed the whole subject of Schubert's life, in every detail, has been so exhaustively covered in dozens of books that it can be safely left until the next lost diary or revealing letter is discovered. Instead there are many areas of Schubert's music which demand more attention than has been the case so far.

It is also to be hoped that the subject of Schubert's occasional anti-social behaviour and drinking habits have been so widely written on that the subject can be laid to rest. It is not the case that even recently published books can be said to reach any consensus on the topic. Indeed, Elizabeth Norman McKay's *Franz Schubert: A Biography*, devotes a whole chapter to the topic,[*] adding the suggestion that Schubert additionally suffered from a separate medical condition which today would be called cyclothymia. This is characterised by cyclic episodes of depression. However, despite this possibility, and despite the well-known effects of syphilis, Schubert, between 1823 and his death five years later, produced an astonishing array of works of the highest originality and beauty which even gave rise to the nonsensical notion (entertained even by the great Vogl) of somnambulism. What is evidenced from a number of sources[†] is the occasions on which Schubert surprised his company by outpourings of profound ideas – surprising to those who had previously thought him a reclusive and taciturn individual. To

---

[*] McKay, 'Two Natures,' Chapter 6.
[†] Anton Ottenwalt letter to Josef Spaun describing an evening with Schubert during a visit to Linz in 1825, *Docs* No 574.

those now familiar with the works composed in those miraculous five years, it is no surprise to discover that Schubert possessed a highly developed intellect which surely gives the lie to any notion that he was the boorish, coarse individual portrayed by some.

Returning to the music itself, first in the list of musical topics for research must be the operas, which continue to be sidelined. Had Schubert had better luck with librettists, theatre managers and impresarios, there is little doubt that he would have studied the initial performances of his operas and made adjustments, cuts and insertions to improve the production and to make the show work on the stage. There is no reason why such measures should not now be applied to the operas, belatedly, to include even Liszt's more radical idea of engaging a poet to rewrite the libretto. Further, the expertise and energy so far devoted to completing the unfinished works for the concert hall could be devoted to the unfinished operas,* a task already in hand to a limited extent.

The missing factor is, of course, public demand. Given the huge cost of staging readily available operas, no project to rewrite or complete a Schubert opera could be viable without audience appeal. However, the presentation need not be in an opera house nor staged with expensive opera stars. Given the unfamiliarity and novelty of the works it is likely, given appropriate marketing in advance, that a relatively modest production could gain sufficient following via an appropriate media platform to justify continuing the process or encourage others to join. At the moment, research activity in the operas is virtually non-existent, despite extensive efforts at least to record all the music. What is needed, in addition to academic study, is a business scheme comparable to the efforts which created (and made money out of) the *Lilac Time* venture. The objective would be

---

* Brian Newbould's suite from *Die Zauberharfe* was performed in Vienna in 2019.

simply to promote and exploit this still new tranche of Schubert's wonderful music.

Doubtless academic research will continue into the finer points of Schubert's music but it should never be forgotten that what did not happen in his lifetime was the development of a serious public following. That following is now a reality for much of his output, certainly for his chamber music and *lieder*. There is no reason why it should not be replicated for the rest of the music, given the right presentation. At least true Schubertians still have much to look forward to.

WHAT IS IT ABOUT SCHUBERT?

To conclude this journey, let us reflect a moment on what makes the music of Franz Schubert so appealing, to the extent that otherwise serious professional people are content to devote time to the study and experience of it. There is no doubt that some have experienced a Damascene conversion upon encountering Schubert's music, an early example being George Grove, who was won over after listening to performances at the Crystal Palace concerts led by Augustus Manns, himself a longstanding convert. Whatever the formula, there will always be new converts who, intentionally or otherwise, become entranced at hearing just one *lied* or one Moment Musical, then search out others and discover the whole world of delight awaiting the explorer into Schubert's music. Is it the melodies that refuse to leave the head, or the drama of the song cycles, or the relentless drive of the last movement of a quartet? Whatever it is, it draws the listener on to demand more, and more there is in great abundance at every turn.

Many have analysed the scores to identify the key ingredients – and have, of course, discovered a world of complexity making up the superficially simple surface of the music. Brian

Newbould, in his recent two-volume *Schubert's Workshop*,* has explored and expounded Schubert's harmonic palette from the viewpoint of one who has not only analysed many of the great works but has taken on the task of completing many of the unfinished compositions, assuming the role of the composer himself. Yet to appreciate and even to understand the harmonic nuances that make up the music is just part of the task. How does one analyse or even describe a Schubert melody beyond the use of words, which immediately seem inadequate to the task? And we must then put the harmony and the melody together, along with the rhythm and the dynamics, often such an important part of the work, to see how all these in combination create the sounds and sensations that fix themselves in the mind. So the search ends as it began, with the realisation that there is something about the music of Schubert that is unique to this genius of two centuries ago, music that through good fortune and the endeavours of a host of enthusiasts has been preserved for us.

This work started out with a death but has proceeded to uncover not just life but surely immortality, to the extent that can exist anywhere in our lonely biosphere. Franz Schubert was a unique spirit who blazed out during his short lifespan, but has bequeathed to us a treasury which, above all, we must share and enjoy, for it is one of the true blessings of our lives.

---

* Routledge, 2023.

BIBLIOGRAPHY

Abraham, Gerald: Schubert Symposium, ed, 1946
Barbedette, Hippolyte: Schubert, Sa Vie, Ses Œuvres, Son Temps, 1865
Black, Leo: Franz Schubert, Music and Belief, 2003
Bostridge, Ian: Schubert's Winter Journey, The Anatomy of an Obsession, 2018
Brendel, Alfred: On Music, 2001
Brown, Maurice J. E.: A Critical Biography, 1958
Brown, Maurice J. E.: Essays on Schubert, 1966
Brown, Maurice J. E.: Schubert, Grove Dictionary of Music and Musicians, 1980
Byrne Bodley, Lorraine: Schubert, A Musical Wayfarer, 2023
Capell, Richard: Schubert's Songs, 1928
Carner, Mosco: Article in Schubert Symposium, 1946, ed Gerald Abraham
Clive, Peter: Schubert and his World, 1997
Coleridge, Arthur Duke: English trans of von Hellborn, Life of Franz Schubert, 2 vols, 1869
Davies, Joe and Sobaskie, James: Drama in the Music of Franz Schubert, ed, 2019
Deutsch, Otto Erich: The Schubert Reader, a Documentary Biography, 1947
Deutsch, Otto Erich: The Schubert Thematic Catalogue, 1951
Deutsch, Otto Erich: Schubert, Memoirs by his Friends, 1958
Dvořák, Antonin: Article in The Century, New York, 1894
Einstein, Alfred: Schubert, The Man and His Music, 1971, trans David Ascoli
Fischer-Dieskau, Dietrich: The Book of Lieder, 1976
Flower, Newman: Franz Schubert, the Man and His Circle, 1928, rev 1949
Freed, Stan: Schubert's Symphony No 7: The Schubertian (SIUK), editions of 2020
Gibbs, Christopher H.: Cambridge Companion to Schubert, ed, 1997
Glazunov, Alexander: Article, Side by side with Beethoven, published by Columbia, 1928
Grove, George: Life of Schubert, Dictionary of Music and Musicians, 1882
Hellborn, Kreissle von: Life of Franz Schubert, 1865
Henehan, Donald: The Dark Side of Schubert, New York Times, 1989
Hutchings, Arthur: Schubert, Master Musicians series, 1945, ed Eric Blom.
Kobald, Karl: Franz Schubert and his Times, 1928, trans Beatrice Marshall
McKay, Elizabeth Norman: Franz Schubert, a Biography, 1996
Messing, Scott: Schubert in the European Imagination, 2007, 2 vols
Newbould, Brian: Schubert and the Symphony, 1988
Newbould, Brian: The Music and the Man, 1997
Newbould, Brian: Schubert's Workshop, 2023
Prod'homme, Jacques-Gabriel: Schubert Raconté Par Ceux qui l'ont Vu, 1928

Reed, John: Schubert, The Final Years, 1972
Reed, Paul: Dear Brown, exchanges between Deutsch and Brown, 1949 to 1967: Schubert Institute Research Centre
Reissmann, August: Franz Schubert, Sein Leben und seine Werke, 1873
Schumann, Robert: Neue Zeitschrift, ed, 1843
Shaw, George Bernard: Music in London, 1890-94, 3 Vols
Solomon, Maynard: Franz Schubert and the Peacocks of Benvenuto Cellini, 19th-Century Music, 1989
Tovey, Donald: Essay on Schubert in A Schubert Centenary, 1928
Wasserman, Janet I.: First Performances, The Schubertian; April 2009 9-21

INDEX

C
Cantatas

Kantate zu Ehren von Josef Spendon, D472 **34**
Namensfeier für Franz Michael Vierthaler, D294 **41**
Stabat Mater, D383 **34**

Chamber music

Octet, D803 **29, 71**
Arpeggione Sonata, D821 **96**
Variations on *Trockne Blumen*, piano and flute, D802 **3**
Violin sonatas (published as sonatinas), D384 385, **408, 153**
Fantasia in C, violin and piano, D934 **153**
Rondeau brillant, violin and piano, D895 **153**

L
Lieder

Adelwold und Emma, D211 **141**
Adelaide (not the one by Beethoven), D95 **161**
Aeschylus, D450 **27, 45**
An Herrn Josef von Spaun, D749 **162, 163**
Alpenjäger, D588 **159**
An die Musik, D547 **87, 222**
Auf dem Strom, D943 **26**
Aus Heliopolis I and II, D753 and 754 **161**
Der blinde Knabe, D833 **207**
Der Hirt auf dem Felsen, D965 **33, 153**
Der Jüngling und der Tod, D545 **159, 163**
Der Leiermann, D911 no 24 **145**
Der Tod und das Mädchen, D531 **16, 23**
Der Wanderer, D493 **23, 53, 70**
Der Wanderer and Der Mond, D649 and D870 **161**
Die Allmacht, D852 **26**
Die Forelle, D550 **17, 20, 83, 159**
Die Nacht, D983 **80**

Die Sterne, D939 **26**
Die junge Nonne, D828 **100**
Die zürnende Diana, D707 **83**
Erlkönig, D328 **14, 57, 100, 159**
Fischerweise, D881 **26**
Geheimes, D717-720 **142**
Gesang der Geister über den Wassern, D704 **80**
Gretchen am Spinnrade, D118 **14, 83, 159, 160**
Gretchen im Zwinger, D564 **141**
Gruppe aus dem Tartarus, D583 **141**
Heidenröslein, D257 **161**
Jägers Abendlied, D368 **159**
Kreuzzug, D932 **26**
Mirjams Siegesgesang, D932 **32**
Morgenlied, D685 **23**
Prometheus, D674 **24, 52**
Schlachtgesang, D443 **26**
Sehnsucht, D656 **80**
Ständchen, D889 **26 141**
Ständchen (*Zögernd leise*), D920 **35, 163**
Stabat Mater, D175 and 383 **142**
Suleika, D720 **142**
Wein und Liebe, D901 **80**
Wiegenlied, D867 **159**

Lieder cycles

Die schöne Müllerin, D795 **19, 23, 78, 159, 165, 166, 221**
Winterreise, D911 **25, 165, 168-70, 173, 210, 221**
Schwanengesang, D957 **26, 159, 165, 170-1, 221**

M
Masses

Mass No 1 in F, D105 **13, 175, 203**
Mass No 2 in G, D167 **80, 175**
Graduale in C, D184 **176**
Salve Regina Offertorium, D223 **176**
Mass No 3 in B flat, D324 **175, 177**
Mass No 4 in C, D452 **175**
Deutsches Requiem in G Minor, D621 **175**
Mass No 5 in A flat, D678 **80, 17**
Tantum Ergo in C, D739 **176**

Deutsche Messe, D872 **40, 175**
Mass No 6 in E flat, D950 **27, 80, 175**

O
Operas

Der Spiegelritter, D11 **178, 184**
Des Teufels Lustschloss, D84 **78, 181**
Fernando, D220 **34**
Die Freunde von Salamanka, D326 **181**
Die Einsiedelei, D337 **79**
Die Bürgschaft, D435 **181**
Die Zauberharfe, D644 **26, 220**
Sakuntala, D701 **193**
Alfonso und Estrella, D732 **26, 51, 67, 83, 76, 182**
Fierrabras, D796 **26, 79, 141, 182**
Der Graf von Gleichen, D918 **78, 183**
Lilac Time **128, 186**

Opera/Singspiel

Claudine von Villa Bella, D239 **141, 181**
Die Zwillingsbrüder, D647 **26, 178**
Die Verschworenen, D787 **85, 179, 181**

Orchestral

Overtüre Im Italienischen Stil, D590, 591 **33, 181**

P
Piano works, solo

Impromptus, D889 **141**
Impromptus, D935 **151**
Moments Musicaux, D780 **151**
Drei Klavierstücke, D946 **155**
Piano Sonata in A Minor, D784 **150**
Piano Sonata in A Minor, D845 **150**
Piano Sonata in D Major, D850 **150, 210**
Piano Sonata in G Major, D894 **25, 150**
Wanderer Fantasia, D760 **23, 31, 74, 79**
Final piano sonatas, D958, 959, 960 **27, 46, 53, 62, 128, 152, 157**
Piano Sonata in B flat, D960 **333-335**
Relique Sonata in C, D840 **150, 220**

Variations dedicated to Beethoven, D624 **151**, **204**

Piano 4-hands

F Minor Fantasia, D940 **18**, **27**, **238**
Grand Duo in C, D812 **78**, **229**, **238**
Lebensstürme, D947 **152**
Piano Fantasia in G, D1 **153**

Piano Trios

Piano Trio in B flat, D898 **25**, **152**
Notturno Trio, D897 **152**
Piano Trio in E flat, D929 **22**, **25**, **26**, **29**, **152**, **236**

Piano Quartet

Adagio and Rondo, D487 **78**

String Quartets

Quartet in B flat, D112 **78**
Quartet in G Minor, D173 **78**
Quartettsatz, D703 **21**, **220**
Quartet in A Minor, D804 **22**, **23**, **99**, **144**
Quartet in D Minor, D810 **22**, **61**, **99**, **144**, **161**, **205**, **210**
Quartet in G, D887 **22**, **26**, **76**

Quintets

String Quintet, D956 **9**, **27**, **53**, **68**, **76**, **107**, **125**, **143**, **209**, **210**
Trout Quintet, D667 **9**, **13**, **125**, **152**

R

Rosamunde, Fürstin von Cypern, Ballet, D797 **22**, **25**, **88**, **144**, **237**

S
Symphonies

Symphony No 1, D82 **95**, **97**, **145**, **193**, **194**, **203**
Symphony No 2, D125 **95**, **97**, **193**
Symphony No 3, D200 **95**, **97**, **193**
Symphony No 4, D417 **95**, **144**

Symphony No 5, D485 **24**, **35**, **95**, **145**
Symphony No 6, D589 **24**, **36**, **47**, **95**, **192**, **195**
Symphonic fragments, D615, D708A **48**, **188**, **196**, **220**
Symphony No 7, D729 **21**, **64**, **95**, **97**, **194**, **197**, **218**
Unfinished Symphony, D759 **22**, **56**, **80**, **87-89**, **107**, **123**, **126**, **204**, **220**
Gastein Symphony **120**, **135-7**, **218**
Great C Major Symphony, D944 **26**, **47**, **61**, **64**, **66**, **67**, **92**, **143**, **204**, **205**, **218**
Tenth symphony, D936A **27**, **138**, **194**, **237**, **240**

ABOUT THE AUTHOR

John Uff's interest in music has spanned a lifetime and taken many forms including playing the piano, violin, viola, trombone and singing and, while his children were growing up, becoming a luthier to make violins, violas and cellos for them to play. His passion for Schubert developed early as a boy treble in the school choir, when something in his music lodged in the mind and has never departed. The question what is it about Schubert has remained intriguing as the answer continues to elude. His later pursuit of books on Schubert and his music led to the realisation that the life of this extraordinary man had left significant gaps, particularly in what happened between his tragically early death in 1828 and the present day. The fate of the music he left, the majority being in manuscripts of which there were often no copies, is an adventure story in its own right.

John is a keen supporter of the Schubert Institute (SIUK) and has assigned all the profits from this publication to their use to further the support of Schubert's music and particularly young performers. His day job as a KC and now as an Emeritus Professor of Law at King's College London have given ample opportunity to further his musical interests, both as Treasurer of Gray's Inn, with its fine musical tradition, and as President of the Bar Musical Society. He has also written plays for a village amateur drama group about the fate of local lads in WWI, a theme that has always fascinated. His many publications on legal issues have also been a useful prelude to writing about music.

www.ingramcontent.com/pod-product-compliance
Lightning Source LLC
Chambersburg PA
CBHW071153070526
44584CB00019B/2772